MARIO LEMIEUX

OVERCOMING ADVERSITY

MARIO LEMIEUX

Tim O'Shei

Introduction by James Scott Brady,
Trustee, the Center to Prevent Handgun Violence
Vice Chairman, the Brain Injury Foundation

Chelsea House Publishers
Philadelphia

Dedication: To Jake Eck: A courageous superstar and Hall of Fame kid. Thanks for sharing your inspiring story . . . T.O.

CHELSEA HOUSE PUBLISHERS

EDITOR IN CHIEF Sally Cheney
DIRECTOR OF PRODUCTION Kim Shinners
PRODUCTION MANAGER Pamela Loos
ART DIRECTOR Sara Davis
PRODUCTION EDITOR Diann Grasse

Staff for **Mario Lemieux**
SENIOR EDITOR John Ziff
ASSISTANT EDITOR Rob Quinn
LAYOUT 21st Century Publishing and Communications, Inc.

First Printing

1 3 5 7 9 8 6 4 2

The Chelsea House World Wide Web address is
http://www.chelseahouse.com

Library of Congress Cataloging-in-Publication Data

OíShei, Tim
    Mario Lemieux / by Tim OíShei
        p. cm — (Overcoming adversity)
    Includes bibliographical references and index.
    Summary: Describes the life and hockey career of Mario Lemieux, Pittsburgh Penguins star.
    ISBN 0-7910-6307-0 (alk. paper)
    1. Lemieux, Mario, 1965- 2. Hockey players—Canada—Biography—Juvenile literature. 3. Pittsburgh Penguins (Hockey team)—Juvenile literature [1. Lemieux, Mario, 1965- 2. Hockey players.] I. Title. II. Series.

GV848.5.L46 O84 2001
796.962'092—dc21
[B]
                                    2001047726

CONTENTS

OVERCOMING ADVERSITY

ON FACING ADVERSITY

James Scott Brady

I GUESS IT'S a long way from a Centralia, Illinois, train yard to the George Washington University Hospital Trauma Unit. My dad was a yardmaster for the old Chicago, Burlington & Quincy Railroad. As a child, I used to get to sit in the engineer's lap and imagine what it was like to drive that train. I guess I always have liked being in the "driver's seat."

Years later, however, my interest turned from driving trains to driving campaigns. In 1979, former Texas governor John Connally hired me as a press secretary in his campaign for the American presidency. We lost the Republican primary to a former Hollywood star named Ronald Reagan. But I managed to jump over to the Reagan campaign. When Reagan was elected in 1980, I was "sitting in the catbird seat," as humorist James Thurber would say—poised to be named presidential press secretary. I held that title throughout the eight years of the Reagan administration. But not without one terrible, extended interruption.

It happened barely two months after the Reagan administration took office. I never even heard the shots. On March 30, 1981, my life went blank in an instant. In an attempt to assassinate President Reagan, John Hinckley Jr. armed himself with a "Saturday night special"—a low-quality, $29 pistol—and shot wildly as our presidential entourage exited a Washington hotel. One of the exploding bullets struck me just above the left eye. It shattered into a couple dozen fragments, some of which penetrated my skull and entered my brain.

The next few months of my life were a nightmare of repeated surgery, broken contact with the outside world, and a variety of medical complications. More than once, I was very close to death.

The next few years were filled with frustrating struggles to function with a paralyzed right side, struggles to speak and communicate.

To people who face and defeat daunting obstacles, "ambition" is not becoming wealthy or famous or winning elections or awards. Words like "ambition" and "achievement" and "success" take on very different meanings. The objective is just to live, to wake up every morning. The goals are not lofty; they are very ordinary.

My own heroes are ordinary folks—but they accomplish extraordinary things because they try. My greatest hero is my wife, Sarah. She's accomplished a lot of things in life, but two stand out. The first has been the way she has cared for me and our son since I was shot. A tremendous tragedy and burden was dropped unexpectedly into her life, totally beyond her control and without justification. She could have given up; instead, she focused her energies on preserving our family and returning our lives to normal as much as possible. Week by week, month by month, year by year, she has not reached for the miraculous, just for the normal. Yet in focusing on the normal, she has helped accomplish the miraculous.

Her other most remarkable accomplishment, to me, has been spearheading the effort to keep guns out of the hands of criminals and children in America. Opponents call her a "gun grabber"; I call her a national hero. And I am not alone.

After a seven-year battle, during which Sarah and I worked tirelessly to educate the public about the need for stronger gun laws, the Brady Bill became law in 1993. It was a victory, achieved in the face of tremendous opposition, that now benefits all Americans. From the time the law took effect through fall 1997, background checks had stopped 173,000 criminals and other high-risk purchasers from buying handguns, and the law has helped to reduce illegal gun trafficking.

Sarah was not pursuing fame, or even recognition. She simply started at one point—when our son, Scott, found a loaded handgun on the seat of a pickup truck and, thinking it was a toy, pointed it at Sarah.

Fortunately, no one was hurt. But seeing a gun nearly bring a second tragedy upon our family, Sarah became determined to do whatever she could to prevent senseless death and injury from guns.

Some people think of Sarah as a powerful political force. To me, she's the person who so many times fed me and helped me dress during my long years of recovery.

Overcoming obstacles is part of life, not just for people who are challenged by disabilities, illnesses, or tragedies, but for all people. No matter what the obstacle—fear, disability, prejudice, grief, or a difficulty that isn't likely to "just go away"—we can all work to make this world a better place.

Pittsburgh Penguins owner and Hall of Fame player Mario Lemieux returns to the ice, December 27, 2000. It was the third time he resumed his career after an extended layoff.

1

SIMPLY
THE BEST

"HAT TRICK." THAT'S what four-year-old Austin Lemieux expected from his dad. Three goals is a pretty steep order, especially for a guy who hasn't played hockey in three and a half years. Austin had never before seen his father play, but he must have heard that his dad had been good, really good. In fact, some might say he was the best in the world.

So on December 27, 2001, the first time Austin would get to see his father play, a hat trick is what he wanted. "The pressure is on!" Austin's father, Mario Lemieux, said a few hours before he would make history.

Some fans were referring to the game as "Super Mario's Return." Forty-four months earlier he had retired after playing 13 seasons and winning two Stanley Cups and six scoring championships with the Pittsburgh Penguins. His jersey number 66 had been retired, symbolized by a huge banner hanging from the rafters of Mellon Arena in Pittsburgh. In the autumn of 1997, just a few months after he retired, Mario was inducted into the Hockey Hall of Fame. Normally a player is not eligible for induction until three seasons have passed since his retirement. Indeed, Mario's status as one of the best players ever to play the game was already secure.

In fact, Penguins fans saw him as something of a savior of their beloved franchise. With the money-troubled owners of the Penguins threatening to move out of Pittsburgh in 1999, Mario put together a deal to buy the club. Once he owned the team, he made it clear that the Penguins would be staying put in the Steel City.

Just one year after becoming an owner, though, Mario was itching to play hockey again. At age 35, with three seasons of rest, he felt young and strong enough to do it. Plus, he had made comebacks before: one from cancer, and another from serious back surgery. But this would be his ultimate comeback, his chance to shine one more time as the finest player in the world.

He had been getting ready for this day for nearly two months. In November, Mario had begun working out. News of his comeback broke in early December. "I will try to regain the title of best player in the world," he had told reporters when he officially announced his intention to play the remainder of the 2000–2001 season, and possibly more.

With the Pittsburgh Penguins ready to face the Toronto Maple Leafs, 17,148 people squeezed into Mellon Arena, and more than a million viewers watched on television as the enormous number 66 banner was lowered and folded. With the Tina Turner song "Simply the Best" blaring from the sound system, the real number 66 stood on the ice and watched as the banner descended and disappeared into a box. Mario's wife, Nathalie, was there with the couple's three daughters (Lauren, Stephanie, and Alexa) along with his mother and father. Austin was standing nearby in the Zamboni entrance. Just before the game began, Mario skated by and tapped his stick on the glass. Austin waved back.

Now it was time for Mario to show his son what it meant to be the best. Lemieux skated to the red line, squared up against the Maple Leafs' center and captain, Mats Sundin,

and hunched over for the opening face-off. As the puck was dropped, Mario Lemieux was officially back in the National Hockey League. A half-minute later, he was behind Toronto's net, the puck on his stick. He threw a pass to Jaromir Jagr, Pittsburgh's captain and star player since Mario had left, who shot the puck past Leafs goalie Curtis Joseph. Just 33 seconds into his comeback, Mario had notched an assist and helped give Pittsburgh a 1-0 lead.

An ear-piercing cheer rose from the crowd for that play,

Fans lined up outside the Mellon Arena for a chance to see Mario return for the Penguins in a home game against Toronto. Mario is the first player/owner in the NHL.

but the volume would only increase later. Halfway through the second period, Mario sprinted down the left side of the ice, skated to the right circle, and yelled over to Jagr to pass him the puck. Jagr did, and Lemieux shot the puck past Joseph. That intensified the cheering to a volume never before heard in Pittsburgh. Even many of the 175 reporters covering the game, usually a quiet (and much smaller) group, were excited. "The fact that he did what he did left even the most hardened of us just shaking our heads in amazement," said Jim Kelley, senior writer for FoxSports.com. "I was sitting there with a lot of people who have seen a lot of hockey, and there wasn't one of them who didn't say, 'I can't believe what I'm seeing.' "

One of the fans who saw the game on television was actor Christopher Reeve, who is most famous for playing Superman in the movies of the 1970s and 1980s. Like Mario, Reeve knows all about overcoming adversity: in 1995, the actor was paralyzed from the neck down after a horse-riding injury. Also like Mario, Reeve has a son, Will, who is a hockey fanatic.

Though they are both New York Rangers fans, Christopher Reeve and his eight-year-old son Will watched Lemieux's comeback game together. By game's end, they admitted that Mario had gotten them interested in the Penguins, too. "We were overjoyed," Reeve said. "As fans of the game, to see him come out there after everything he's been through, and it was only a couple of months to get back in shape, it was a tremendous act of courage. We were thrilled to see that. So now whenever the Rangers are not playing but the Penguins are, we always tune in to watch Mario. He's a real hero."

During his first game back, Mario went on to record another assist as the Penguins won, 5-0. A three-point evening wasn't exactly the same as the three goals Austin had hoped for, but it was enough. (In the National Hockey League, points represent a player's offensive statistics. With assists and goals being worth one point each, Mario's game of two assists and a goal gave him three points for his comeback game.) Everyone, from the players to the fans to Austin himself, was dazzled by Mario's performance. After the game, Austin ran into the dressing room, smiling wide and pointing at his father. "I saw you," he said. "I saw you!"

Mario grew up in the birthplace of hockey, Montreal, Quebec. The sport is as big a part of Canadian culture as baseball once was in the United States.

2

THE HALLWAY STAR

IF MARIO LEMIEUX'S life was a mystery, if nothing was known of his childhood, nobody could make up a story to top the real one. The actual version of Mario's life is more dramatic than a Hollywood movie.

As a child, he was a hockey phenom at the same age that he was learning to write in cursive. He was scouted by one of the greatest hockey men in history (and, incidentally, his future Penguins coach) before he was even in high school. When Mario was too young to cross the street on his own, his mother and father built a skating rink atop the carpet inside their home. When people hear that, they don't believe it. But it's a true story, and face it: Who could possibly make up something like *that?* Like many parts of Lemieux's life, it's beyond imagination. People just don't *do* that.

But Mario Lemieux has always done the things that others can't do.

When he was born on October 5, 1965, he was already the best. In French—which is the language Mario spoke growing up in Montreal,

Quebec—the words *"le mieux"* mean "the best." So from the moment he was born to Pierrette and Jean-Guy Lemieux, he was "Mario the Best."

The Lemieux's house, in the suburban town of Ville Emard, was located about 10 minutes away from a skating rink called the Forum in Montreal. With the arena of the NHL's Canadiens within walking distance, Mario was never far from his ultimate destiny: the National Hockey League.

Hockey's origins are actually rooted in Montreal. The history of the sport traces back to 1875, when the first organized hockey league began play in Montreal. Since then, the sport has been like a religion in Canada. Everybody watches, talks about, and plays the game.

So, like most people in Canada, Jean-Guy and Pierrette were hockey fans. Before their three sons were born, they often bought tickets to Canadiens games at the Forum. Jean-Guy was a construction worker; Pierrette was a housewife who kept busy raising the three Lemieux boys. The first, Alain, was born in 1960, five years ahead of Mario. Richard was born in 1963, and Mario, the youngest, came along a year and a half later.

Growing up, Mario was a shy boy. Except for his family, he didn't have a lot of friends. While other kids might want to go out and play or just hang out, Mario preferred to sit home and play video games—unless, of course, he had the chance to play hockey. All three Lemieux boys played plenty of hockey. Alain was a forward, and Richard was a defenseman. Along with Mario, they got their start in skating inside their very own house. Lots of cold, fresh snow covers the ground during the long Canadian winters. Pierrette used that snow to clean the rugs inside her house. While cleaning the rugs one day, she got an idea: Using the snow, she could create a miniature ice rink for her three little sons! Pierrette brought in a few shovelfuls of snow and dumped it on the living room rug. She packed it down

and opened up all the doors and windows to make the house icy cold. Pierrette and Jean-Guy strapped their sons' tiny feet into their skates and let them trudge around the hallway and living room.

As the boys got older, they played more and more on real ice rinks. The closest was located right across the street, behind St. Jean de Matha Church. Young Mario could often be seen playing there until nine or ten o'clock every night.

Pierrette Lemieux, seen here with her son Mario in 1997, supported the hockey aspirations of all three of her sons. She literally turned her carpet into a skating surface when the boys were very young.

Hockey was simply a priority in the Lemieux household, and nothing got in the way. One night, the boys' 16-year-old cousin was babysitting them. Alain, Richard, and Mario wanted to watch *Hockey Night in Canada,* which is broadcast every Saturday evening and is considered a don't-miss program amongst fans. Their cousin changed the channel and refused to switch it back to *Hockey Night.* Frustrated, the boys waited for her to use the bathroom. When she did, they locked her inside and put the game back on. They wouldn't let her out until the broadcast was over.

When he was six, Mario started playing organized hockey for a team called the Hurricanes. He wore jersey number 27, the same as Alain. Quickly, Mario realized that he had an extra helping of talent. As a young player, around age eight, Mario frightened a goalie right out of the crease! He reared back, ready to unleash a hot slap shot, but before Mario could whack the puck, the goalie scooted out of the crease. With the net wide open, Mario relaxed and gently flipped the puck into the goal. (Later, Mario and the goalie, Carl Parker, became teammates on the peewee Hurricanes.)

Even as a kid, Mario was blessed with an obvious talent for seeing everything that was happening on the ice. In practice, Mario once left a drop pass for a teammate he hadn't seen. Afterward, someone asked Mario how he knew his teammate was there. He explained, "I could tell by the sound of his skates."

Playing in youth leagues while he was in elementary school, Mario regularly scored more than 100 goals in a season. Word spread quickly around the province of Quebec that a future superstar was playing for the Ville Emard Hurricanes. Crowds started gathering to see Mario. One year during a championship game, over 5,000 people came to see him play.

To stop Mario, other teams would often take cheap shots at him. After games, it wasn't unusual for Mario to have a couple of black eyes and slash marks covering his body. But he gave out some punishment, too: sometimes he would retaliate, which caused him to lose ice time in the penalty box. Once, after Mario was charged with several minutes in penalties during the first period of a game, his coach sat him out for the second. With the team down 6-1 entering the third period, Mario apologized and was put back into the game. He scored six goals, leading his team to a 7-6 comeback win.

Mario had very high expectations for himself, and pushed himself hard. Between the ages of 10 and 14 his youth coach was Ron Stevenson. Like a teacher handing out a punishment for poor behavior, Stevenson had players do things such as write "I must not take bad penalties" numerous times. Seeing this, Mario decided to discipline himself. Without his coach even telling him to do it, Mario made himself write "I must work harder on back-checking."

When Mario was 13 years old, he was scouted by the already-legendary coach of the Montreal Canadiens, Scotty Bowman. One day, Bowman would coach Lemieux to a championship with the Pittsburgh Penguins. If somebody had told him that at the time, Bowman might even have believed it. He could tell that this kid was good. "I saw him play when he was 13," Bowman told reporters years later. "I was coaching the Canadiens, and he was playing a peewee league in Montreal. He was the best I ever saw at that age. . . . With Lemieux, you always knew. Even when he was 13."

Ron Stevenson knew Mario was going to be a teenage celebrity and, probably before he reached age 20, an NHL star. Knowing that such stardom carries with it a lot of responsibility, Stevenson coached Mario in politeness and people skills. Because he was shy, Mario didn't naturally go out of his way to smile and greet people warmly when he met them. It wasn't that Mario didn't like people; it simply wasn't in his

Wayne Gretzky raises his arms after scoring a goal on Toronto goalie Paul Harrison. While still in youth leagues Mario was already being compared with "the Great One."

nature to shake hands and be talkative with those he didn't know.

When Mario was 14 or 15, he began being compared with another young Canadian who was nearly five years older. Wayne Gretzky, who would eventually win six Stanley Cups with the Edmonton Oilers in the 1980s, was becoming known as hockey's greatest superstar ever. Most people felt Mario was just behind him, and might one day be even better. There was one difference—and this comes back to Stevenson's off-ice coaching: Gretzky was likable and personable. People thought he could serve as a symbol for hockey, an exciting, friendly athlete who made the sport more popular around North America and even the world.

Now, it appeared Mario Lemieux might be able to do the same thing.

Mario's talent on the ice was obvious from a young age. A stubborn streak would become the only question mark scouts had about the future superstar.

3

THE NEXT GREAT ONE

EVEN WHEN HE was a young teenager, people knew Mario Lemieux was destined to be an NHL star. But before he could get there, he had to perform at the next level. In Canada, the training ground for the pros is the junior hockey level. Currently there are three leagues at this level: the Western Hockey League (WHL), Ontario Hockey League (OHL), and the one in which Mario played, the Quebec Major Junior Hockey League (QMJHL).

Most Canadian boys with enough talent get signed to junior contracts at age 15 and have to leave home to play in another city. In their new town, they will live with a local family (called a "billet") that will be responsible for feeding, transporting, and supervising them. Mario was lucky. In the 1981 midget draft, he was picked first overall by the Laval Voisins, which were located just outside Montreal. To play in Laval, he didn't have to travel far at all.

Junior hockey players are paid a small stipend (Mario got $65 a week) to cover expenses such as food. Just like professionals, they can be traded to other cities or cut. But unlike pros, they travel by bus from city to city in the dead of the Canadian winter. In other words, playing junior hockey was not a glamorous life.

Having Mario in the league, however, was about to make junior hockey in Quebec a lot more exciting. When he was signed, Mario promised to revive the struggling Voisins by winning the QMJHL scoring title and leading the team to a championship. Certainly, the hopes of the Voisins' fans were pinned on this superstar named Lemieux.

In light of the expectations, Mario's first season with the Voisins was a disappointment. The team finished in the middle of the league standings, and Mario finished 17th in scoring with 96 points. The Voisins were selling more tickets, and fans were excited to see Mario, but he wasn't happy with the results. He didn't even win rookie of the year; that award went to another future NHL star, Pierre Turgeon, who had scored 23 fewer points than Mario that season.

Thinking about what he could do to improve his performance, Mario came to a tough conclusion: he decided to quit school. That way, he figured, he could spend more time practicing and getting himself ready for games. Without attending classes during the day and doing homework at night or in the mornings, Mario knew he could focus totally on hockey. Everyone already knew that Mario was headed to the NHL, so he was confident that he didn't need a diploma or degree to get a job. And, if for any reason hockey didn't work out, Mario knew he could always return to school and graduate when he was older.

Pierrette and Jean-Guy Lemieux were always supportive of Mario's hockey, but his dad really didn't want his son to quit school. Only after a lot of convincing did Jean-Guy agree to give Mario his blessing to drop out. With that, Mario ended his schooling after completing the 10th grade.

During the 1982–83 season, Mario scored a superhuman 84 goals and recorded 184 points in 66 games. But, unbelievably, that wasn't enough to win the scoring championship. In December, Mario had left Laval to join the Canadian national

Dave King, head coach of Canada's national junior team in 1982, didn't like Mario's work ethic. He benched the budding star more than once during the championships.

junior team in the Soviet Union. The 1982 world junior championships were being held in Leningrad, and Mario would be there for two weeks.

At first, he had been eager to play on the national junior team. But Mario quickly found that he didn't get along with the coach, Dave King, who thought that Lemieux didn't work hard enough on defense. Because of this, King used Mario sparingly, even benching him for some games.

Though he managed to notch five goals and five assists in 10 games, Mario hated the experience.

Meanwhile, back in Quebec, he was getting beaten in the QMJHL scoring race by an American rookie named Pat LaFontaine. Playing for the Verdun Junior Canadiens, LaFontaine scored 104 goals and 234 points in 70 games. The Voisins were the best team during the regular season, with a 53-17-0 record. But they lost in the semifinal round of the playoffs.

During the summer of 1983, Mario worked harder than ever to prepare himself for the season. This would be his final year of junior hockey; he would be eligible for the NHL draft in the spring of 1984. He wanted to be the first player taken, so he cut back on his off-season golf and started working out both on and off the ice.

The extra work paid off. Mario tore through his final season, smashing all his previous goal totals and even surpassing LaFontaine's astronomical mark from the year earlier. By the end of the 1983–84 season, Mario had scored 133 goals and 282 points, erasing the record that Guy Lafleur (130 goals) had set in 1970–71. If anyone had doubted Mario's marketability as the top amateur player for the pro draft, they didn't anymore.

What some people did doubt was his attitude. Sometimes Mario appeared too laid back on the ice, as if he were gliding around for fun. Other people defended him, saying that he was such a natural talent that he had an effortless skating style. Controversy was also a part of his final junior season: When Mario was again picked to play in the World Junior Championships in December, he refused to join the team. He said he wanted to stay and play for the Voisins, who had a good chance at winning the Memorial Cup as the league's top team. He also wanted to chase the scoring title. "I've been thinking about my decision for a long time, since we came back from the tournament last year," he said. "It was very tough to play in the league after. I was tired. It hurt my game."

The QMJHL said that Mario would be suspended from playing in league games during the junior tournament if he didn't go. Believing that the decision was unfair, Mario took the league to court and asked the judge to block the QMJHL's decision and allow him to play. The judge agreed and issued a permanent injunction that made it impossible for the league to suspend a player for refusing to play in the world junior tournament. Taking the league to court as an 18-year-old showed that Mario was not afraid of controversy and was willing to stand up for what he believed. Some people admired his confidence, calling it a gutsy move. Others thought he was being petty and babyish, not to mention disloyal to Canadian hockey.

Mario responded by saying he was being loyal to his team by staying to play. He kept playing for Laval and went on to do exactly what he had hoped: win the league scoring title and break Guy Lafleur's one-season goal record of 130. With one game remaining, he needed three goals to reach 130 and tie Lafleur. With Gretzky in the stands watching (the Oilers were on a road trip in Montreal), Mario scored six goals. He ended the regular season with 133 goals and 149 assists for 282 points. Mario's only other quest was to lead Laval to a Memorial Cup championship. In that quest, he failed: the Voisins were eliminated three games into the championship tournament.

The superhuman accomplishments Mario made during his final year in junior hockey also heated up comparisons with Wayne Gretzky. Five years older than Mario, Gretzky was already established as a scoring champion playing for the Edmonton Oilers while Mario was playing in junior hockey. Both players shared the same agents, Gus Badali and Bob Perno, and had even met at a charity golf tournament in Toronto. That was in August 1981, just before Mario's rookie season with Laval. Gretzky took Mario to the filming of a commercial, then out to dinner on Yonge Street in Toronto. That night, Gretzky reportedly gave

Mario poses with his idol and 1997 All-Star teammate, Wayne Gretzky. The two first met in 1981, and Gretzky offered the younger Mario advice on handling his soon-to-arrive celebrity.

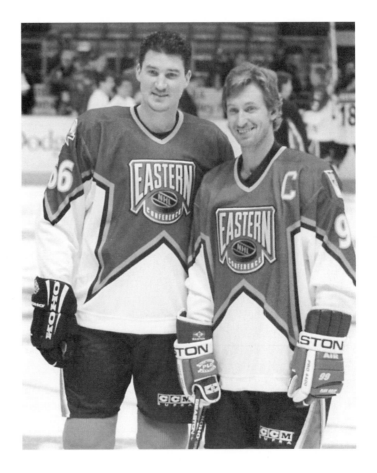

Mario some insight on things he would be dealing with as a pro, like contracts, commercial deals, and handling the many people who would approach him with business deals. "[Gretzky] is his idol," Badali said. "That first time they met, Mario was in awe of Wayne."

Mario is famous for wearing number 66, a number he chose in Laval. Gretzky, of course, wore number 99. People have always speculated about whether Mario picked the jersey number 66 because it is 99 upside-down. Mario has denied that, but in any case, he and Gretzky would be forever linked by much more than their uniform numbers. Beginning in the early '80s, they were mentioned together in conversations among hockey analysts and fans from all over. Back then, the question was simple: Who would be better—Gretzky or Lemieux? Everyone had an opinion. Mario was bigger and, many people thought, had a tad more natural talent. Gretzky, on the other hand, seemed to have more ability as a leader. He was more energetic and enthusiastic when doing interviews or meeting fans.

Back in the early 1980s hockey was struggling to establish itself in North America as one of the four major sports. One of the ways a sport becomes popular and respected is for its best athletes to become household names. In other words, people in homes across America would know who Wayne Gretzky was, even if they weren't hockey fans. Within hockey, it was hoped that Mario could reach that same level of recognition.

But people were getting nervous. If Mario did things like refuse to play for a national team and take his league to court, he couldn't be a celebrity spokesman for the game. What he was about to do at the NHL draft after being picked by Pittsburgh didn't help, either.

Mario Lemieux was a sure-shot superstar. Everyone agreed that he would be a great player. But would he be good for hockey?

There was no sure answer to that.

A young Mario stands with his mother at the announcement of his new contract with the Pittsburgh Penguins. Upon being drafted he was seen as a savior of the franchise.

4

THE TOP PICK

SOMETIMES, BEING THE worst team in the league isn't so bad. For the Pittsburgh Penguins, it was at least a familiar position. From the time they joined the NHL in 1967 until the 1983–84 season, Pittsburgh had been consistently bad. Only nine times had the Penguins made the playoffs, and in only three of those playoff appearances did they advance beyond the first round.

In 1983–84, the Penguins' 16-58-6 record made them the NHL's worst team. But few people seemed to mind that poor distinction. First, the Penguins had averaged 6,839 fans per game in Civic Arena (now known as Mellon Arena). They were losing money *and* games; there was even talk of moving the team to Hamilton, Ontario. In a Pennsylvania steel town with a football mentality, Pittsburghers were hardly concerned about the Penguins' poor fortune.

Secondly, those people who were Penguins fans found some solace in their last-place status. Being the worst team in hockey gave the Penguins the right to pick first in the NHL draft on June 9, 1984. For

Eddie Johnston, the man charged with running the Penguins, that was good news. For three years, he had tracked Mario Lemieux's junior hockey career and had watched the young French Canadian man play. Now, Johnston was going to pick him to do much more than play for the Pittsburgh Penguins. Johnston knew that Mario could save the Penguins. "Mario Lemieux," he said, "is the best player in the draft, by a mile."

Even while Mario endured a string of controversies during his junior career—taking the league to court, not getting along with King, being accused of laziness—Johnston stuck by his man. "You just don't have those kind of skills, to do the things he can do with the puck," Johnston said. "It doesn't matter what level you're at. Then I watched him do it in the Memorial Cup. People said he was lazy and things like that, but I saw him take the puck twice and go right through the whole team and I said, 'Ooooh.' It was a very easy decision."

Johnston had plenty of offers to deal away the top pick in the draft to another team, which could then take Mario. Some of the offers were attractive: simply for giving up Mario, who was then a teenager and unproven at the pro level, Johnston could get several solid players and a star. That would improve the Penguins' roster immediately, probably even quicker than simply landing Lemieux. But Johnston said no.

Two teams that were under special pressure to trade for Lemieux—the Montreal Canadiens and Quebec Nordiques—were both from French-speaking Quebec. French Canadians are particularly proud of their heritage and like to see their own succeed, preferably at home. So it was no surprise that many fans from the Province of Quebec wanted to see Lemieux end up there. The teams felt that pressure, too. "It's an opportunity that arrives maybe once every 10 years," said the president of the Quebec Nordiques, Marcel Aubut. "Our scouts are unanimous that he's the closest thing to Gretzky. He's also a guy from our neighborhood and that's why you have to do everything you can to make sure [a trade] is doable."

The general managers from both Montreal and Quebec told Johnston to give them a call if the other team made an offer for Lemieux, because they would match it. "Montreal said if we were going to trade him to Quebec," Johnston said, "to come back to them before we made the deal, that they would more than match the deal."

Other teams were just as interested. The Minnesota North Stars offered all 12 of their draft picks to Johnston just for Lemieux. If he wanted, Johnston could have named his price for Lemieux and gotten it. But he said no to everyone. He wanted nothing but Lemieux. "I was very emphatic I was not going to do anything," Johnston said.

When draft day finally arrived, representatives from every team in the league gathered in the Montreal Forum. So did reporters, fans, and eligible junior players and their families. The Lemieux family was one of those in the stands; of course, their home was only 10 minutes away, which made the day all the more exciting. Not only was Mario going to be drafted number one overall in the NHL, he was going to get that honor in front of a hometown crowd.

It surprised no one when Johnston stood at the podium and proudly announced, in French, that the Pittsburgh Penguins were picking Mario Lemieux. What happened next was a little surprising and, to many observers inside the Forum, quite upsetting. It's a draft day tradition in the National Hockey League that players put on the jersey of the team that just picked them over their shirt and tie and pose for pictures. Following the advice of his agent, Gus Badali, Mario refused to join the Penguins' management, wear the jersey, or pose for any pictures. The reason was that Mario and his representatives were unhappy with the way contract talks were progressing with the Penguins. Badali and Johnston had begun talking about the details of a contract a few weeks earlier and still were not close to agreeing on financial terms. "I didn't go to the table because the negotiations are not going well," Mario told reporters. "I'm not going to put on the sweater if they don't want me bad enough." (Years later, Mario admitted that he regretted not posing for pictures with his new jersey.)

The fans in the Forum were outraged, and reporters expressed their anger with negative columns. "Lemieux acting like a petulant prima donna," read one headline. Despite the bitter beginning, it did not take too long for Mario and the Penguins to reach agreeable terms. One week later, he agreed to a contract worth approximately $700,00 over two years, making him the best-paid rookie in NHL history at the time.

With Mario now officially part of their franchise, the Penguins began using his name and image to entice the people of Pittsburgh into buying tickets. Pittsburgh's most popular sports team had always been the National Football League's Steelers, who had been epitomized by quarterback Terry Bradshaw. Mario Lemieux, the Penguins hoped, could be their Terry Bradshaw.

The Penguins advertised the first home game in the fall of 1984 as the "Lemieux Debut." But catchy phrases will never do more to attract sales than actual superstar feats, and Mario provided one of those in his first seconds as a Penguin. The team opened the 1984–85 season on the road in Boston, playing against the Bruins. During Mario's first shift, he blocked a shot by Boston defenseman Ray Bourque and carried the puck down-ice. Mario now had a breakaway on Bruins goaltender Pete Peeters. As he carried the puck along the ice, even Mario was surprised that this was happening. When he came up close to Peeters, he followed his instinct and shot.

That shot was the first of his shift, his first of the game, and the first of Mario's career. The goal that followed, of course, was also the first of his NHL life.

Mario Lemieux would always accomplish things in quick and glamorous style. His first game at Civic Arena in Pittsburgh came on October 17 versus the Vancouver

Canucks. On his first shift, Mario registered an assist on a goal by Doug Shedden. Later in the game, he had his first fight in the National Hockey League, against Vancouver's Gary Lupul.

The Pittsburgh skyline. Despite a rocky initial reception, Mario was quickly embraced by the Steel City.

While Mario's professional career started well on the ice, he was struggling away from it. Having grown up speaking French, he was now learning to speak English. Before going to Pittsburgh, he had taken a Berlitz intensive English-language course, spending five hours per day for

Mario celebrates after scoring his first goal—on his very first shot in the NHL. The date was October 12, 1984; the victim, goaltender Pete Peeters of the Boston Bruins.

three weeks in the class. It helped, but not enough. Reporters bombarded Mario with questions after nearly every game, and almost all of them spoke English. That meant that Mario's struggle with the English language was broadcast for the world to hear. Every time he made a mistake or couldn't come up with exactly the words he needed to express what he was feeling, there were cameras, microphones, and notepads recording it. Because of his discomfort with the language, along with his natural shyness, Mario didn't like doing interviews.

To help himself learn the language, Mario watched television soap operas during the daytime. He also got help from the family of Tom and Nancy Matthews, with whom he lived during his first year. Eddie Johnston, knowing that Mario would be adjusting to many different kinds of pressure during his rookie season, arranged for him to live with the Matthews family. Tom and

Nancy, who were friends of Johnston and his wife, Diane, had three sons who had left home for school. "All three of our sons had played hockey and they were about the same ages as Mario and his brothers," Nancy Matthews told the *Pittsburgh Post-Gazette*. "Eddie was aware of the similarities and he thought we would be a perfect place for Mario."

Nancy cooked for Mario, took care of his laundry, helped him find his away around Pittsburgh, and basically did everything a mother would do. Even in his second season and beyond, when Mario lived with his girlfriend and future wife, Nathalie Asselin, Nancy would check on the couple.

Mario's first season was an astounding success. He piled up 100 points, including 43 goals, which earned him the NHL's Calder Trophy as Rookie of the Year. He was picked to play in the midseason All-Star Game and earned MVP honors. Pittsburgh didn't make the playoffs that year, but the Penguins did improve from previous seasons. And even better, people who followed hockey had a gut feeling that the Pittsburgh Penguins' fortunes were changing. With Mario Lemieux carrying the club, things were going to get better. It wouldn't happen right away. In fact, it might not even happen in the first few years. But people suspected—no, they *knew*—that one day, Mario Lemieux would lead the Penguins to a trophy they had never seen before: the Stanley Cup.

Mario himself knew that it would take a while for the Penguins to become a winning team. Even he couldn't provide a quick fix; it takes more than one superstar to make a championship team. So while Mario stacked up scoring milestones, the Penguins struggled through the mid-1980s.

In 1985–86, his second season, Mario put together a 28-game point streak, scoring 21 goals and 38 points between January 11 and March 15. The next year, he scored over 100 points for the third season in a row. Mario was unquestionably living up to the expectations that he would be a star, but he and the Penguins had yet to score the goal they really wanted: making the playoffs.

At practice with Team Canada during the 1987 Canada Cup, Mario waits for Wayne Gretzky to relace his skates. Mario learned a great deal watching Gretzky perform day-in and day-out.

5

ON THE
WORLD STAGE

MARIO LEMIEUX WANTED to be a winner. He wanted to prove to people that he could play under pressure and lead his team to a championship. With the Penguins' poor records the first few years of his career, Mario had no chance to do that. Other than playing in the world championships in the spring of 1985 and helping lead Canada to a bronze medal, Mario had become accustomed to having his hockey season end early. May through August were months for golf, not chasing the Stanley Cup or any other championship.

That changed in the summer of 1987. Prior to the start of the NHL season, in August and September, the best players from around the world gathered in Canada. There they played for their countries in an international tournament called the Canada Cup. With all the NHL players available, it was easy to predict which teams would be among the best. Team Canada was stocked with superstars, the biggest two being Wayne Gretzky and Mario. The Soviet Union team was also guaranteed to be great: with the cold war and communism still going strong, the Russian team was a mysterious hockey machine. Their players weren't allowed to play in the National Hockey League, but they were certainly good enough. Tensions always grew high when the Soviets played Canada, and this tournament would be no different.

Mario would also be spending five weeks learning how to be a leader and a superstar. Gretzky got more media attention than anyone else, and Mario watched the way he handled it. Gretzky made a habit of smiling and joking with reporters, keeping things relaxed and friendly. The reporters appreciated the easygoing rapport they had with hockey's biggest star, and having the media on his side made Gretzky's life easier, too.

Watching Gretzky practice also provided valuable lessons. With or without the puck, he always pushed hard and competed during practice. Especially for superstars, who can be good even when they're not giving 100 percent, it's easy to relax a little during practice. Fairly or not, Mario had been accused of doing just that during his first few years in Pittsburgh.

But Gretzky's teammates—and Mario in particular—saw that he was always fighting for the puck, skating hard, and encouraging his fellow players. Most people who know both men agree that watching and working with Gretzky for five weeks was one of the greatest lessons of Mario Lemieux's career.

"Of course, we had all played against Wayne and knew how great he was," said Ray Bourque, a Team Canada teammate and a Boston Bruins defenseman at the time. "But what we didn't know and the thing that impressed, maybe even surprised everyone, was how hard he works. All that talent, and he competes with such intensity every shift. He made us all better with his example, and for a young player like Mario, it is a great experience to be around him for a long stretch and see how the number one guy operates, especially how he never, never coasts."

At the beginning of the tournament, Team Canada coach

Mike Keenan wouldn't play Gretzky and Mario on the same line, except on the power play. He had wanted to spread out his offensive power. But by the time Team Canada reached the championship round, a best-of-three series against the Soviet Union, Keenan considered the idea. Canada lost the first game, 6-5, which meant they had to win games two and three. In the second game, Keenan played Gretzky and Lemieux together in the second period. It was a magical match: Mario scored two goals before the end of the third. With the score tied, the game went into sudden death. In the second overtime period, Mario scored to even the series and send it to a third and deciding game.

The lead in game three bounced back and forth, with Valery Kamenski tying the score at 5-5 with a goal for the Soviets. With less than two minutes remaining in the third period, Keenan sent Mario, Gretzky, and Dale Hawerchuk (all of whom would one day be in the Hall of Fame) onto the ice. Hawerchuk won the face-off and dumped the puck to Gretzky, who carried it up the left side of the rink. Mario was skating behind Gretzky, waiting for a pass. Here, Gretzky had a choice to make: he could take the shot himself, hold the puck and keep moving, or pass it to Mario. "Playing with Gretzky," Mario said after the tournament, "you just find some open ice and he finds you with the puck."

That's exactly what happened. Giving up his own chance to be the hero, Gretzky sent the puck back to Mario. After receiving the pass, Mario relied on his instinctive sense of timing. He waited a moment, then unleashed a high shot that plunked into the corner of the net.

With that goal, Team Canada had won the championship. "For me, that probably still ranks as the greatest hockey game I ever saw in person," said Jim Kelley, a hockey writer for FoxSports.com who has covered the game since the early 1980s. "To me, Gretzky giving Mario the puck in the Canada Cup that year for the game-winning goal against the Russians, that's an unselfish act

Mario lifts Wayne Gretzky as the two celebrate Mario's Canada Cup–winning goal, September 13, 1987.

that elevated Mario on the world stage. . . . Wayne could have taken that shot."

Mario was now a champion. His next step was to do it again, but this time with his own team and for the Stanley Cup. In the 1987–88 season that followed the Canada Cup tournament, Mario did what he could by dominating the National Hockey League with 79 goals and 98 assists for

168 points. All three marks were Penguins records, as were his 22 power play goals. For his accomplishments, Mario won the Art Ross Trophy (given to the league's top scorer) and the Hart Trophy (awarded to hockey's most valuable player). He had also been named MVP of the All-Star Game for scoring three goals and adding three assists in a victory for his squad.

The only problem was, even in the most outstanding season of Mario's young career, the Penguins failed to make the playoffs. The team finished with a record of 36 wins, 35 losses, and 9 ties. That totaled up to 81 points, which had the Penguins finishing 12th out of 21 teams. They were sixth in the Patrick Division, having just missed a playoff spot.

But there was good news. The Penguins had finished with a winning record. Mario was playing better than ever. Soon, very soon, the fortunes of hockey in Pittsburgh had to change.

Entering the 1988–89 season, the Penguins were finally able to surround Mario with a solid supporting cast. He would lead his team to the playoffs that season.

6

CHASING
THE CUP

MARIO LEMIEUX WAS learning to deal with superstardom, and he was happy to be doing it in Pittsburgh. He knew that if he played in a hockey-crazed city like Montreal, he would never have any privacy—especially as a French Canadian. "It's kind of hard to play in Montreal," Mario said early in his career. "You have a lot of pressure from the media and the fans. They know their hockey and it's harder on a player when you're from Montreal."

Mario was growing more comfortable with the English language, but he remained a shy, private person. He also remained focused on making the playoffs.

Finally it happened. In the 1988–89 season, the Penguins had a stronger lineup that included a line of Mario, Rob Brown, and Bob Errey, who combined for 160 goals. Their second center, Dan Quinn, scored 34 goals. Defenseman Paul Coffey, a Canada Cup teammate of Mario's who was acquired in a trade with Edmonton, scored 30 goals and tallied 83 assists. In short, the Penguins had plenty of firepower to use against opposing goalies, and the results earned them a second-place finish in the Patrick Division. In the first round of the playoffs, the Penguins swept the New York Rangers. That was Pittsburgh's first victory in a playoff series since 1979. Round two versus the Philadelphia Flyers went to seven games, and this time the result wasn't so positive: the Flyers won game seven, 4-1. Saddening as that outcome was, Mario and the Penguins were encouraged. They were playing well, having dominated the first playoff series and playing tough to the end in the second. "I know I'll drink from the Cup one day," Mario said, "I just know it."

Mario had good reason to believe. His teammates were playing well, and he had shattered his own records. He scored 85 goals that year, including 5 in one game on December 31 versus New Jersey. That night, he scored every kind of goal a player can: one at even-strength, one on the power play, one short-handed, one on a penalty shot, and one into an empty net. That same year, Mario also recorded 114 assists, giving him 199 points and making him the winner of the Art Ross Trophy as the league-leading scorer.

Traditionally, the top scorer was also the most likely candidate for the Hart Trophy as the league's most valuable player. After the season ended in 1989, Mario expected to win it. When the votes were announced, however, it turned out that Wayne Gretzky was the winner. Gretzky had been traded to the Los Angeles Kings and led his team to the playoffs.

"I think the ultimate insult to Mario from the media was the year that he was the scoring champion, dominated the league, and Wayne got the Hart Trophy for guiding the Los Angeles Kings into the playoffs," said writer Jim Kelley, who worked for the *Buffalo News* at the time. "For years, essentially, if you were the best scorer in the league, you were also the best player. Somebody unearthed the phrasing that said, 'Player judged to be most valuable to his team' and used that to swing a lot of votes towards Wayne.

I think [Mario] was really bothered by that. I think that's when he actually first realized that personality comes into play as well as ability."

It would be years before Mario was to match Gretzky's role as a spokesman and salesman for the game of hockey. He would have many more challenges to meet first, the first of which would present itself the very next season. The Penguins began the 1989–90 season in a streaky, stumbling style. Losing 14 of their first 26 games was enough to get head coach Gene Ubriaco and general manager Tony Esposito fired. One man, Craig Patrick, was hired to fill both jobs for the remainder of the season.

For his part, Mario began the 1989–90 season explosively. He embarked on a scoring streak that began in October and spanned the entire months of November, December, and January, in which he scored a goal or dished out an assist in every game. The streak was big news; everywhere the Penguins played, all eyes focused on Mario to see whether he would extend his streak.

For as well as he was playing, Mario was feeling awful. Sometime around the first of the year, his back began to ache. Soon the pain became unbearable; it got so bad that Mario couldn't even bend over to tie his skates or shoes. For about 20 games, he played through the pain. But on February 14, during a game against the New York Rangers, Mario decided that the pain was too severe and too alarming. He ended the streak at 46 games and flew to California to see a doctor who specialized in back treatment. Mario spent the next six weeks working with Dr. Robert Watkins's staff in Los Angeles, trying to rehabilitate his back without going through surgery. With all the promise the Penguins had shown one season earlier, Mario desperately wanted to return to the team and do his part to help the team make another playoff run.

While Mario worked out in southern California, the Penguins played a lot of tight-scoring games. They entered the final game of the season with 72 points in the standings. One more point would be enough for Pittsburgh to squeeze into the playoffs, so the Penguins needed to tie or beat Buffalo in their last regular season game. After skating in L.A., Mario felt strong enough to return for that final game in Buffalo. He registered a goal and an assist to help tie the game at 2-2, but Buffalo scored in overtime to win the game and end Pittsburgh's season.

That summer, two major operations took place that would affect the fortunes of the Penguins. One was on Mario's back. Further testing showed that surgery would be the best way to correct his problems. On a July day in Pittsburgh, doctors opened Mario's back and removed a herniated disc. "There were lots of nights that I tossed and turned in bed and couldn't even sleep because I would feel a sharp pain running up and down my spine," Mario said. "Then after the surgery, I couldn't play golf without having it bother me again. I couldn't bend over to line up a putt." Maybe Mario wouldn't be playing golf that summer, but doctors predicted he would be ready for training camp.

The other operation that happened in Pittsburgh during that off-season was performed by the Penguins' front office. Patrick kept his job as general manager but hired a man named "Badger" Bob Johnson to be the Penguins' new head coach. A longtime coach at the University of Wisconsin and a former director of USA Hockey, Badger Bob had a reputation as a positive, encouraging coach who excelled at motivating his players.

Patrick also hired one of the most successful hockey men in history, Scotty Bowman, to be the Penguins' director of player development. As a head coach with St. Louis, Montreal, and Buffalo, Bowman had won five Stanley Cups. In stark contrast to Badger, Bowman was known as a stern taskmaster who rarely smiled. But his success as a hockey man was unmatched. "That's a pretty impressive front-end team they've put together in Pittsburgh," said Glen Sather, who, as general manager

Scotty Bowman and his impeccable track record were brought to Pittsburgh in the summer of '90.

of the Edmonton Oilers, led a team that won five Stanley Cups in the 1980s.

Things had never looked better for the Penguins. They had a top front office. They had a strong lineup that now included strong contributions from Mark Recchi and Kevin Stevens. Their new young superstar from the Czech Republic, Jaromir Jagr, was said to be the next Mario. And the dazzling superstar himself was about to return. Or so everyone thought.

On a preseason trip to Houston for an exhibition game, Mario felt an excruciating pain in his back. He tried to exercise and stretch it out, which only made the throbbing pain worsen. When doctors stuck a needle in Mario's back to do tests, they discovered that he had a rare infection. If not treated properly, the infection could spread to the bones and spine. Mario spent the next three months resting on his back, unable to do much of anything. He didn't talk to reporters during that time, making his condition a mystery of sorts. "The doctors discovered an infection in my back and treated it some more," Mario told *The Sporting News* during the following season. "It got better, but I knew then that this was something that might never go away, never be 100 percent again. I learned to trust the doctors and rely on them. I want to keep playing this game as long as I can play up to the standards I've set so far. I don't want to be all crippled when I leave this game."

At the beginning of January 1991, Mario was finally given permission to begin skating. His teammates had been playing well enough to keep the Penguins in the playoff race. By the time Mario returned in late January, the Penguins had won 26 of their 50 games. In his first game back, on January 26 in Quebec, Mario recorded three assists in a 6-5 win.

Playing up to his usual standards was no problem: not then, nor at any other point in his career, did Mario's performance crumble. But from 1991 on, it took extra-special care to get Mario ready for games. Every morning, he would lay on a table and receive a half-hour of back treatment from the Penguins' medical staff. If there was a game that night, he would get more back treatment in the afternoon. Tying his skates was a unique challenge: from time to time, the act of bending over to lace the boots would wrench Mario's back so badly that he couldn't play. That problem was easily solved: An equipment man laced Mario's skates for him. The Penguins also constructed an angled wooden stool that helped Mario tie his own skates when he felt he could. "I'm sure people don't realize just what he goes through to go out there and entertain them night after night," said winger Rick Tocchet, who didn't join the Penguins until a year after Mario began following this detailed pregame routine.

"I've seen him grimace when he pulls up his pants and heard him groan when he pulls his jersey over his head. He has a doctor, two trainers and two equipment men helping put him together, so to speak. Then we see him go out there and dominate the game the way Michael Jordan dominates basketball. Amazing."

While Mario struggled simply to get dressed, the Penguins spent February losing enough games to convince Patrick to pull the trigger on a six-player trade. He sent John Cullen, Zarley Zalapski, and Jeff Parker to the Hartford Whalers for Ron Francis, Ulf Samuelsson, and Grant Jennings. Francis brought some veteran leadership and scoring ability; Samuelsson was a tough player who excelled at getting under the skin of opponents. That addition proved to be a perfect fit for the Penguins, who used a late-season surge to finish first in the Patrick Division.

Pittsburgh's first opponent in the playoffs was the New Jersey Devils. The series was close, extending all the way to seven games before the Penguins won it with a 4-0 victory in Pittsburgh. Washington was the second-round opponent; the Penguins beat the Capitals in five games.

To get to the Stanley Cup Finals, Mario and his teammates had to win one more series—this one against the Boston Bruins. The first two games were played in Boston, with the Bruins winning both. But by now, the Penguins were confident enough not to give up. In fact, Kevin Stevens even guaranteed that Pittsburgh would come back to win the series. "I'm saying right now, we'll beat this team," Stevens said. "I can't wait to play [game three] Sunday night."

Stevens was right. The Penguins won the next four games, and they did it convincingly: Each margin of victory was by two goals or more. With their momentum at full speed, the Pittsburgh Penguins were going to play in the Stanley Cup Finals. "Winning the Stanley Cup," Stevens said, "would be the ultimate thrill."

Pittsburgh's opponent was the Minnesota North Stars

Mario finally hoists the Stanley Cup on May 25, 1991, after the Penguins defeated the Minnesota North Stars in the best-of-seven series, 4-2.

(the same franchise that is now the Dallas Stars). The Finals opened in Pittsburgh, with the North Stars winning the first game and the Penguins taking the second. The series then moved to Minnesota for game three. Before the game, Mario hunched over to tie his skates and experienced back spasms. He had to sit out, and the North Stars won game three to take the series lead, 2-1.

Mario returned for game four and the Penguins won the next two, entering game six in Minnesota with a 3-2 advantage. One more win and the Cup would be theirs. One more win and the precise reason Mario had been brought to Pittsburgh would be realized.

Every year, every team shoots for the Stanley Cup. It had been 24 years since the Penguins were born into the National Hockey League, and they had never won—or even seen—the Stanley Cup. It's a tradition that the winners of the Cup sip champagne from it. After waiting 24 long years for a taste, the Penguins were parched. So with all their guts, with all their thirst, the Pittsburgh Penguins burst into game six. Samuelsson scored first, Mario second, and it went from there. By game's end, the score was 8-0.

The Stanley Cup belonged to Pittsburgh.

Mario's back felt fine that night as he hoisted the Stanley Cup above his head. "No strain at all," he said. "This is the ultimate dream."

Mario competes against Wayne Gretzky in 1992. Despite a tumultuous beginning, the 1991–92 season would be another championship year for the Penguins.

7

WINNING IT
FOR BADGER

THE SUMMER OF 1991 should have been a joyous one—the best ever—for the Pittsburgh Penguins. Players who had been with the team during the lowly days of the 1980s, guys who had felt as though they were stranded and starving on a desert island, had been rescued and delivered to paradise. No trophy in hockey is more special than the Stanley Cup, and now each player for the Penguins was getting his name engraved on it permanently. The Pittsburgh Penguins ruled the world of hockey. After so many years of failure, to be a champion felt great.

That's why when the team got some bad news in late August, it felt as if a thief had stolen the Cup in the middle of their party. It was news nobody ever expected to hear and nobody could have possibly imagined.

On August 30, 1991, the Penguins announced that Bob Johnson had malignant, or cancerous, tumors growing on his brain. The news left the players, who cared for Johnson deeply, searching for words. "I saw him about a week and a half ago," Mario said. "He was the same old

Badger everybody knows. It's scary. Really sad."

Johnson was too sick to coach and had to undergo immediate treatment. During the preseason, assistant coaches Rick Kehoe, Rick Patterson, and Barry Smith ran the team together. Meanwhile, the thoughts, energy, and prayers of the Penguins were fully with Bob Johnson. "What he's done for this city and this hockey club in one year is pretty incredible," Mario said. "Nobody thought we'd win the Cup, but with Bob Johnson, anything was possible."

The last time Johnson saw his team skate was on September 19, when the Penguins played an exhibition game in Denver. General manager Craig Patrick, meanwhile, was waiting until the last possible moment to name a head coach. When he finally made a decision, it came one day before the start of the regular season. The pick was a natural one: Scotty Bowman, the most successful coach in hockey history.

Bowman's style was completely the opposite of Johnson's, sort of like the difference between playing for a drill sergeant or for your grandfather. "Bob cared about you off the ice as well as on the ice," Mark Recchi said later in the season. "With Scotty, you're lucky to get a hello out of him." Still, the players knew that Bowman was a winner. They also knew that the best thing they could do for Bob Johnson was to win another Stanley Cup. Anything less would be considered failure.

The 1991–92 season began in decent—but certainly not spectacular—form, with the Penguins winning 10, losing 8, and tying 2 of the first 20 games. What jolted them was the news that came on November 26, the day when the Penguins' worst fears were realized. That day, when the players came into the locker room after practice, Patrick told them that Johnson had died that morning. Saddened and shocked, nobody talked. For 15 minutes, the players sat frozen in place.

The next night, the Penguins had a home game against

"Badger" Bob Johnson is seen here while he was still coaching the Penguins. Though he succumbed to cancer in November 1991, his spirit stayed with the team through the 1991–92 season.

the New Jersey Devils. To honor Johnson, the team had his famous phrase—"It's a great day for hockey"—painted on the ice next to both blue lines. Before the face-off, the players gathered in a circle on the ice while fans held up electric candles as a singer sang "The Lord's Prayer."

Inspired, the Penguins went on to beat the Devils, 8-4. From that point onward, the Penguins were especially determined to win a second Stanley Cup. They won 10 of their next 14 games, trouncing their opponents in almost every victory. They beat the Philadelphia Flyers by a score of 5-1. They beat San Jose, 8-0, and 12 days later, by a 10-2 score. Toronto fell victim, 12-1; Washington fell, 6-2. In the month after Badger died, the Penguins soared like never before.

But things soon changed. In January and February, the Penguins struggled mightily, losing 14 of their 24 games. Everyone was frustrated—Bowman because he felt several players weren't working hard enough, and the players because they were unhappy with Bowman's tough, often cold coaching style.

Sensing that some change was needed, Patrick pulled off a three-way deal with Los Angeles and Philadelphia on February 19. The trade brought in four new players, including forward Rick Tocchet, and injected some badly needed life into the Penguins. During the playoff stretch, Pittsburgh won 11 of its 17 games in March and April, finishing the season third in the Patrick Division.

Their first playoff series pitted them against the Washington Capitals. Pittsburgh fell behind three games to one, but managed to come back and win the series in seven games.

In the second round, the Penguins faced the New York Rangers. Pittsburgh won the first game, but disaster struck in game two when Rangers forward Adam Graves slashed Mario in the glove while the Penguins were on the power play. Mario felt a throbbing pain and had doctors look at his hand. After the examination, they delivered news nobody wants to hear during the playoffs: Mario's hand was broken, and the Penguins would have to play on without him.

Though Mario said nothing, in Pittsburgh people reacted angrily to the slash. Suspended for four games, Graves was apologetic and insisted he had not meant to hurt Mario. "When you're penalty killing, you try to put pressure on the guy's hands to move the puck, for him to give up the puck so you can shoot it down the ice," explained Graves, who in the years since has become known as one of hockey's finest gentlemen. "It wasn't an intent to hurt him. In no way would I want to hurt him. I tried to hit him in the gloves, where all the padding is."

Mario was expected to be out for about a month, maybe more. But after the Penguins won game five to take a 3-2 lead in the series, Jagr told reporters that Mario would be back for the next series. It turned out that he was right: the Penguins won game six to eliminate the Rangers and advance to the conference finals against Boston. Pittsburgh won the first game against the Bruins, 4-3, in overtime. Mario was able to return for game two on May 19, just 14 days after his injury. The Penguins won that game, 5-2, and the next two games by a score of 5-1 in each game, to sweep the series and advance to their second straight Stanley Cup Finals.

This was a familiar place for Mario and his teammates, so they knew exactly what they needed to do to win the Cup. Not to mention that the Penguins club of 1991–92 was versatile enough to win any type of game. Some hockey games become high-flying, with the puck zipping all around the rink and lots of scoring. With sharpshooters like Mario and Jagr, the Penguins could play that type of game. But they were equally adept at the opposite style: when the scoring became tight and strong defense was key, Pittsburgh could keep the puck close and under control.

In the 1992 Stanley Cup Finals versus the Chicago Blackhawks, the Penguins used a little bit of both styles. The series started in Pittsburgh, where two periods into the first game, Chicago had a 4-1 lead. In the third, the Penguins surged to tie the game at four apiece. Then, with 18 seconds remaining in regulation time, Blackhawks defenseman Steve Smith was whistled for hooking

*Once reluctant to give inter-
views, Mario happily talks to
the media after the Penguins
secured their second straight
Stanley Cup in May 1992.*

Mario. Chicago coach Mike Keenan didn't like the call:
he thought Mario had purposely fallen to trick the referee into calling the penalty. Keenan grew even angrier
when, five seconds into the power play, Mario knocked a
rebound past Blackhawks goalie Ed Belfour to win the
game for Pittsburgh.

Even though Keenan had been head coach of the
championship Canada Cup team led by Mario five years
earlier, he was incensed at the star now. Before game

two, Keenan blasted Mario with accusations of taking fake dives and stumbles, saying that the star was trying to draw the referee into calling penalties against the Blackhawks. "I can't respect Mario for diving," Keenan told reporters. "The best player in the world is embarrassing himself and embarrassing the game."

Most people thought Keenan was trying to draw attention to Mario's stumbles and put pressure on the officials to call fewer penalties in game two. Whatever the case, Keenan's words didn't seem to affect Mario, who scored the winning goal in the Penguins' 3-1 victory. When someone asked him to respond to Keenan's accusations after the game, Mario said, "No comment—for now."

The question of whether or not Mario was flopping to try to draw penalties continued as the series moved to Chicago. "We don't mean to cast anything negative toward Mario," explained Darryl Sutter, a Blackhawks' associate coach. "We're just asking the question: 'Is there another set of rules, unwritten rules, that are there for Mario and Mario alone?' Based on what we've seen in this series, the answer is yes."

By the time game three was finished in Chicago, there wouldn't be much of a series left to see. Pittsburgh won that game, 1-0, and also took game four in a scoring-fest, 6-5.

With that, the Pittsburgh Penguins were repeat champions. For the second straight year, Mario and his teammates hoisted the Stanley Cup and circled the ice. "When you win once, people wonder," said Kevin Stevens. "When you win twice, it's no fluke."

As they skated the Cup around Chicago Stadium, the Penguins remembered and honored Badger Bob Johnson. For many, only one thing could have made this moment better—the presence of Badger Bob Johnson.

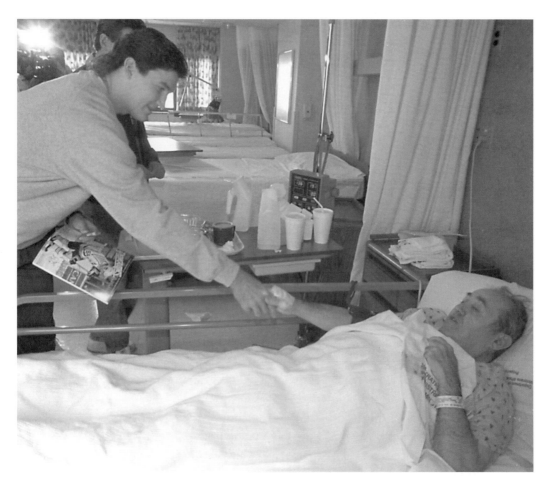

In October 1993, Mario shakes hands with a patient at the Veterans Hospital in Pittsburgh. Just 10 months before, Mario had been a patient battling cancer.

8

THE BIGGEST BATTLE

BEFORE MARIO LEMIEUX was a Stanley Cup champion, back when he was simply a superstar battling a back problem, he had found a helpful way of looking at things. A two-year-old girl named Ashley, who was the daughter of his teammate Tom Barrasso, was suffering from cancer. At the same time that Mario traveled to Los Angeles in 1991 to have doctors treat his back problems, Ashley was at a clinic in southern California fighting her cancer. Mario always told himself things could be worse. His back problems were nothing compared to what Ashley was facing.

The deadly disease was one Mario was growing to know well. Ashley fought cancer and beat it. Penguins coach Bob Johnson died from it. Mario knew others who had passed away from the disease: two uncles, a cousin, and his agent's sister-in-law. But Mario himself had never expected to deal with it. That's why when he noticed a small lump on his neck in 1991 he didn't pay it much attention. About a year later, however, he noticed that the lump had grown and decided to talk about it with the

Penguins team physician, Dr. Charles Burke. When the player and doctor met in December 1992, Dr. Burke wasn't overly alarmed but suggested that Mario have it checked out. So, in early January, Mario had the lump examined by a private physician. Doctors removed the lump, which had formed around a lymph node in his neck. The lump was tested, and the results were shocking. Mario had cancer.

On January 12, 1993, he learned of the diagnosis. The lump had been analyzed and was found to be malignant. The type of cancer Mario had is called Hodgkin's disease, which is named after the English doctor, Thomas Hodgkin, who first described it in 1832. Hodgkin's disease affects the lymph nodes, which help the body pass fluids between the circulatory system and tissues, and also fight disease. Hodgkin's disease enlarges the lymph nodes, which are clustered around the neck (where the first signs of cancer are usually found), armpits, and groin. Males in their late teens, twenties, and thirties form the largest group of people affected by Hodgkin's. Mario, at 27 years old, was right in the middle of that age group.

Not all the details were bad. Four levels of Hodgkin's disease have been identified; Mario had stage one Hodgkin's, which is the least severe and has a 95 percent cure rate. Considering that, Mario's prognosis was good. Still, he was terrified. The day he learned of his cancer, he drove home from the doctor's office dreading the moment when he would see his soon-to-be-wife, Nathalie. (The two had a wedding date set for June.) "After they gave me the news, I could hardly drive between the tears and the crying," Mario remembered. "That was certainly a tough day in my life. I got home. Nathalie was there. I was trying to avoid her. Finally, I had to tell her, but it took a long time for me to say the word, like 20 minutes. I was crying like a baby. She was real nervous. Every time I started to tell her, it wouldn't come out."

Over the next three days, Mario talked about the disease with his family, doctors, and the Penguins' management and players. At that point, he was leading the league in scoring

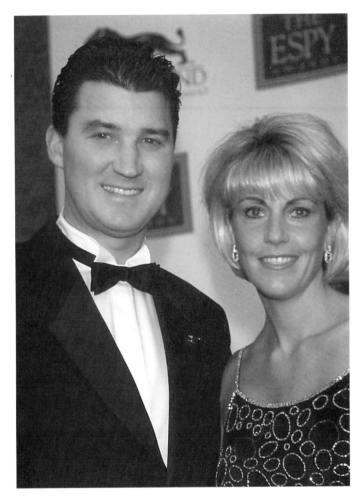

Mario with his wife, Nathalie, at the 2000 ESPY Awards. After learning that he had Hodgkin's, Mario struggled to tell Nathalie.

and was on pace to break Wayne Gretzky's single-season point record. His hockey season would be put on hold so he could spend the next four or five weeks undergoing radiation treatment to kill any remaining cancerous cells in his neck. When he finally commented publicly about his cancer on January 15, Mario described the reaction of his teammates. "I walked into the room and everybody was silent," Mario said. "That's not like our team. It was tough for everybody. I wasn't sure what to say, and nobody else knew what to say. I've had the same experience, talking to people with cancer and not knowing what to say except, 'Good luck.'"

One thing Mario's teammates made clear was that they were more concerned with Mario as a person than as a player. Obviously, it hurt the team to lose its superstar for any amount of time, but the Penguins' players were in no hurry to see Mario play. He had led them to two Stanley Cups while playing through excruciating, arthritis-like back problems. They could only imagine the pain and guts such leadership demanded, and for that they were grateful. What the Penguins' players were extremely eager to see and hear about was a healthy, cancer-free Mario. "I don't know what more that guy is going to have to go through," said forward Troy Loney. "I just feel for him. I couldn't care less when he comes back, just that he gets healthy."

The talk was that Mario might be able to return within four to six weeks, after his radiation treatment was concluded and most of the side effects had subsided. Some people who battle Hodgkin's disease actually continue working while undergoing treatment, but not professional athletes. Mario's excellent physical condition would likely help him to recover quickly, but he would have to wait until his treatment was finished to play.

In late January, Mario began his radiation treatments at the Medical Center in Beaver, Pennsylvania. He continued to visit the clinic throughout February and into early March. During that time, the hospital staff did its best to keep Mario's presence a secret. They didn't tell reporters that he was coming there, and they had Mario wait for treatment in a private room instead of the public waiting room. Mario did take time, however, to visit the children's ward, where he signed autographs and posed for pictures with the kids.

During a four-and-a-half-week period, Mario underwent 22 radiation treatments that bombarded the cancerous area with X-rays and electrons. He lost three or four pounds during that time, which is not considered a lot for people undergoing such treatment. Temporarily, Mario lost his sense of taste. He also had a small bald spot on the back of his head, but was able to comb hair from the top of his head

U.S. Olympic wrestler Jeff Blatnick (right) battles Sweden's Thomas Johansson during the 1984 Olympics. In 1982 Blatnick had received the same diagnosis Mario would later face.

to cover it. "He's done extremely well, much better than I would have forecasted," Dr. James Hughes, director of radiation oncology at the center, told the *Beaver Times*. "It's probably a function of his age, his physical fitness and his desire."

Desire burned brighter in Mario than any disease or injury. When Mario's cancer was first announced, reporters started telling the story of Jeff Blatnick. A world-class Greco-Roman wrestler, Blatnick had been diagnosed in 1982 with the same kind of Hodgkin's that later surfaced in Mario. After being treated with radiation, he began training again. Against the predictions of many experts, Blatnick qualified for the 1984 Olympics and led the United States team to a gold medal. He was diagnosed with cancer a second time in 1985, and almost made the Olympics again in 1988. "I don't live with a cloud over my head," Blatnick told reporters. Mario took the same attitude. On the same day that he finished radiation treatment—March 2, 1993—Mario boarded an afternoon flight to Philadelphia, where the Penguins were playing the Flyers.

That night, having undergone radiation treatment just 12 hours before, Mario played 21 minutes in the game. He scored a goal and had an assist, and though the Penguins lost, 5-4, nothing could have been more encouraging. "It's unbelievable," Penguins left winger Kevin Stevens said. "It's crazy. How can you even imagine what he did tonight? There's only one person in the world who could do it, and it's him."

What got Mario through the fear of facing a killer disease, including more than a month of numbing treatment, and helped him find the will to play as soon as it was over? The answer, according to the people who knew Mario best, was his own resolve. Tom Reich, who is Mario's longtime agent and personal friend, told the *Pittsburgh Post-Gazette* how Mario's bravery inspired the people around him. "You would think some of us who are close to him and who are a lot older than him would give him strength during this hour of need and trepidation," Reich said. "But that was not the case. We gained strength and drew strength from his courage."

Courage is something Mario had displayed all his life. Growing up, he was the youngest of three very competitive brothers. As a youth hockey player he was always the best, which made him a bull's-eye for cheap shots. His young adulthood began by being drafted as the savior of a franchise in a country whose native language he could not even speak. A brilliant career had been hindered many times by stabbing back pain. All of those things, in their own way, require courage. To face and beat cancer simply demanded the strongest, toughest courage Mario could muster. But to him it was simply a part of life. "If you don't have courage, you're not going to beat it," Mario said. "It's my nature to fight back."

Mario returned from his battle against cancer with a flourish. The Penguins went on a 17-game winning streak, and, despite missing 22 games, Mario took the league scoring title.

9

A STAR RETIRES

MARIO LEMIEUX MAY be the only professional athlete in history to beat cancer and win a scoring title in the same season. When he returned in March 1993, Mario was behind Buffalo Sabres star Pat LaFontaine by 17 points in the scoring race. But for both Mario and the Penguins, the rest of the regular season was spectacular. Mario collected points at the pace of a kid collecting toys on a shopping spree in Toys 'R' Us, including a five-goal game against the New York Rangers.

The Penguins, meanwhile, put together a 17-game winning streak at the end of the season, setting an NHL record. Despite missing 22 games, Mario finished the 1992–93 season with 160 points and the scoring championship. With 56 wins and 119 points, the Penguins had enjoyed their best season ever and a first-place finish.

So dominating were the Penguins that virtually everyone in hockey expected them to win a third straight Stanley Cup. The excitement around Pittsburgh was electric, spreading everywhere and to everyone.

In the first round, Pittsburgh easily dismissed the New Jersey Devils in five games. But in the second round, the New York Islanders gave the Penguins an unexpected challenge, forcing the series to a deciding seventh game in Pittsburgh. As the third period ended, the score was locked at 3-3. When the Islanders' David Volek scored in overtime, he not only won the series for New York, he also managed to suck the energy right out of Pittsburgh's hockey dreams. No Stanley Cup. No "three-peat." And as it turned out, there would be no Mario Lemieux for a while, too.

Over the summer of 1993, Mario had corrective surgery performed on his back. Combined with the aftereffects of radiation and cancer, the surgery drained most of his strength. A sense of fatigue caused Mario to miss most of the 1993–94 season. He played just 22 games, and the Penguins were defeated in the first round of the playoffs by Washington.

That summer, after talking to doctors who told him that the only way to overcome fatigue was rest, Mario decided that he would sit out the 1994–95 season. "It's been very difficult the last couple of years," he said, "but I want everybody to know I still love the game of hockey. It's not a hockey issue, it's a health issue."

When asked if he would consider coming back for the playoffs, Mario said no, that this was a season-long decision. To cope with the loss of Mario, the Penguins acquired Luc Robataille from the Los Angeles Kings, signed three centers, and locked up Jaromir Jagr with a long-term contract. Eddie Johnston, who had taken over for Scotty Bowman as head coach, still felt good about his team's playoff chances. But owner Howard Baldwin also knew that fans would be incredibly disappointed over Mario's absence. Reluctantly, he even offered to refund season ticket money for people who didn't want their seats with Mario not playing. "There's no question we'd all love it if Mario could play," Baldwin said, "and nobody would love it more than Mario."

Mario said he wanted to return in the fall of 1995, but

there were no guarantees. His return would depend upon his health. "I don't want to come back until I can play the way Mario Lemieux can play," he said. "If I feel I'm not able to go on the ice and be close to 100 percent, another decision will have to be made."

During the first part of the season that he sat out, Mario felt awful. The fatigue was still ravaging his body in November and December of 1994, and at that point he felt as if he would never play again. But as the season progressed, the rest started to work. Slowly, Mario began to feel better physically. Mentally, he was feeling more and more excited about the prospect of playing hockey again, especially after watching the Penguins beat the Capitals in the playoffs. Plus, his wife, Nathalie, was urging him to continue playing. She didn't want her husband to retire—not yet.

Over the summer, Mario began training by working his lower body on a stationary bike and, for the first time, lifting weights to strengthen his upper body. Feeling stronger, he began seriously training for his comeback. Hearing that Mario Lemieux was working in a weight room during the summer surprised some people who knew him well. One veteran teammate, Ron Francis, told a reporter how Mario used to view off-season training: "We were sitting around after the first Cup and sort of rehashing the season and I asked him if he worked out in the summertime. He said yes. I was actually very surprised and asked, 'What do you do?' He answered, 'Well, starting August 1, I don't order French fries with my club sandwich.' That was his version of conditioning."

Now, Mario's idea of conditioning was to come back in superb shape and prove that, at age 30 and with two serious health problems behind him, he could still play hockey. His first game back happened in Pittsburgh on October 7, 1995. The Penguins were playing the Toronto Maple Leafs. That night, after missing hockey for 18 months, Mario recorded four assists in an 8-3 win. "I was really nervous for the last couple of days. I didn't know how to approach the game, really," Mario said. "It was exciting to get back on the ice and get the ovation again. I've had a few comebacks here in Pittsburgh, but it's always special to come back and share that great relationship with the fans and players."

Mario planned to play 70 games that season, which is exactly what he did. He scored his 500th NHL goal on October 26 against the Islanders in New York. His 161 points were enough to win the fifth scoring title of his career, and the Penguins did well, too, winning their division and advancing all the way to the conference finals before losing to Florida. Overall, the season was a success. But Mario again was chronically tired, and as he later admitted in his autobiography, came within inches of retiring that summer. "I was very close to not playing in 1996–97," he wrote, "closer than most people know." Again, Nathalie Lemieux urged her husband to play one final year. So did his close friends. Only in the two weeks before training camp did Mario decide to return for one final season.

One of Mario's personal highlights that year came on February 4, 1997, in Pittsburgh. On that night, Mario scored his 600th goal. It came on an empty-net shot with 56 seconds remaining against the Vancouver Canucks. When the puck crossed the goal line, the crowd erupted into a standing ovation for Mario. Hundreds of people tossed hats onto the ice in tribute. "That's why I wanted to do it tonight," said Mario, who planned to sit out the next night's game in Montreal to rest his back. "To get a standing ovation like that is something special."

It took Mario 719 games to get his 600th goal, which was one step faster than Wayne Gretzky. (It had taken Gretzky 720 games to do the same.) The score also put Mario in a select group of players who had recorded both 600 goals and 800 assists. The only other players to do that were Gretzky, Gordie Howe, Marcel Dionne, and Phil Esposito. "It's nice to see number 66 get number 600,"

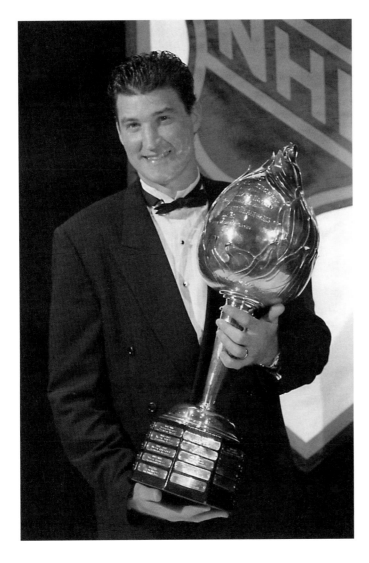

Mario holds the Hart Memorial trophy after being named the league MVP in June 1996.

said Eddie Johnston, who was Pittsburgh's coach that year. "That's terrific. You tend to press and want to get it over with as soon as possible, so it's great for it to happen on home ice."

Though many people suspected 1996–97 would be Mario's final season, he didn't announce that until early April. By that time, he was certain. The Penguins had been streaky through the season, playing well enough to finish second in the Northeast division, but certainly not dominating. Mario scored 122 points (50 goals, 72 assists) in 76 games, winning his sixth scoring championship. Even that wasn't strong enough to convince him to ignore his physical pain or renew his drive to play hockey. After the Penguins were eliminated in round one of the playoffs by Philadelphia, Mario did the expected and retired. He was frustrated with the clutching and grabbing that was dominating hockey and slowing down the game in open ice. "I won't miss the refs, that's for sure," he said. "I won't miss the way the game's being played. But I'm going to miss the guys the most. Being a part of a family for eight, nine months out of a year, spending time with them on the road. . . . That's something I've been doing for 13 years. Once that's gone, that's the biggest thing I'm going to miss."

His own family was something Mario was no longer going to miss. Quite the opposite, actually. Mario was eager to spend more time with Nathalie and their three children: Lauren, Stephanie, and Austin. (A fourth, Alexa, was on the way.) A year earlier, Austin had been born prematurely and almost died. Mario wasn't with Nathalie in the hospital when that happened, which he deeply regretted. "My son almost died in childbirth last year," he said, "and I was away doing my job. A part of me was always with my wife and Austin, but I couldn't help feeling I should have been there more for them."

Golf and travel were part of Mario's plans, but hockey was not. Except for playing in the occasional old-timer game, Mario insisted he would not be wearing skates. "No," he said when asked if he'd skate on his own. "Not at all."

When Wayne Gretzky found out Mario was retiring, he talked about how Mario might not get due credit. "I'm not sure Mario is going to get the accolades he deserves, especially from outside the game," he said. "But from within, the players, the people who follow it closely, realize what he's brought to the table, exactly what he has done."

Gretzky, who was playing for the New York Rangers at

the time, also reminded people that it was Mario who saved hockey in Pittsburgh. "People tend to forget," Gretzky said, "hockey was dying in Pittsburgh before he got there. I played there; it was almost dead. I'm sorry, but the NHL would not have a franchise in Pittsburgh today had Mario not come along. Think about it, no hockey in Pittsburgh."

Though Gretzky's comments were reflecting on the past, it turned out that he was predicting the future, too. Slowly, Mario would begin getting full credit for all he had accomplished. Nobody knew it at the time, but his story was far from complete in 1997.

After retiring in 1997, Mario (right) planned to work on his golf game. Michael Jordan (center), Wayne Gretzky (left), and plenty of other high-profile celebrities were happy to indulge Mario's hobby, showing up for the Toyota Mario Lemieux Celebrity Invitational golf tournament in 1999.

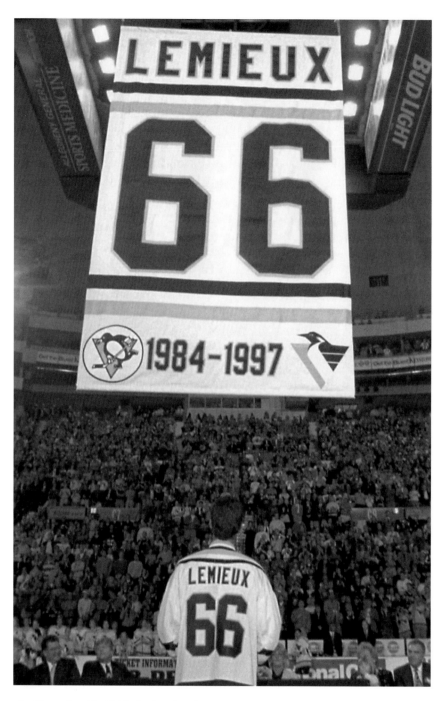

On November 19, 1997, the Pittsburgh Penguins lifted Mario's number to the rafters. No one knew then that "number 66" was a long way from being done with hockey.

10

BUYING
THE TEAM

WHEN A PLAYER retires from the National Hockey League, he must wait three years until he is eligible to be elected to the Hockey Hall of Fame. Yet nobody was surprised when the Hockey Hall of Fame made a special exception for Mario Lemieux. On November 18, 1997, just months after his retirement, Mario was inducted in a ceremony at the Hall in Toronto. Hundreds of fans drove five hours north from Pittsburgh to stand outside the Hall of Fame and cheer as Mario gave his three-minute acceptance speech. "I am grateful that I had a chance to fulfill my ultimate dream of winning a championship for the Pittsburgh Penguins," Mario told the audience during the ceremony.

One night later, Mario felt how grateful Pittsburghers were to him. On Wednesday, November 19, 1997, Mario's jersey number 66 was retired. A huge banner was raised to the ceiling of Mellon Arena, which was packed with a sellout crowd. Mario was showered with gifts. His former teammates chipped in to buy him an expensive addition to his wine collection, a five-magnum bottle of cabernet sauvignon, with a custom-made box. Penguins owners Howard Baldwin and Roger Marino gave Mario a gold medallion, and they made a $250,000 donation to the Mario Lemieux Foundation. (Mario and Nathalie had started the foundation to raise money for cancer and other medical research.) Baldwin and Marino also gave a charm bracelet to Nathalie, gold necklaces to Lauren, Stephanie, and Alexa, and a plaque to Austin.

Standing on the ice, Mario took a microphone and addressed the crowd. "The Hall of Fame was certainly special for me," he said, "but I think tonight is a very special night because I played here for so many years. . . .

"One thing I want to say, for sure: Thank you for making the last 13 years the best years of my life."

Four times during the ceremony, the crowd erupted into standing ovations. During Mario's speech, somebody yelled, "We love you, Mario!"

He looked up, smiled, and answered, "Love you, too!"

That night, Mario talked about how he would want to be remembered by Pittsburgh hockey fans. "Somebody who took a last place team and was able to win a championship seven or eight years later," he said. "That was a big challenge for me when I came to Pittsburgh. I was starting with the worst team in the National Hockey League and was able to persevere, hang in there and finally bring the championship to the city."

At the time, that was exactly the way fans thought they would remember Mario. He had made it clear that his future plans were to stay away from hockey and lead a private life with his family. For the most part, nobody expected to hear much from number 66. Like most legends, he would become a pleasant memory, nothing more. Teenagers at the time would grow up to tell their own kids that they saw Mario Lemieux play.

That's what people expected, but it wasn't to be. Mario would remain in the news, but now the stories would be about lawyers and contracts, not goals, assists, or surgeries.

Back in October 1992, Mario had signed a seven-year contract worth $42 million. The money was guaranteed, meaning Mario would be paid whether he played, got hurt, or even retired. When he did retire in 1997, the Penguins still owed him most of that contract, roughly $30 million. Though Howard Baldwin, the man who had agreed to Mario's deal in 1992, still owned part of the franchise, he now had a partner. In May 1997, Boston businessman Roger Marino had bought a share in the Penguins equal to Baldwin's. (The sale came about because the team was losing money and needed the extra cash.) When he bought in, Marino also took control of the team's finances.

Now, a year later, Mario and his agent, Tom Reich, believed that Marino was deliberately trying to avoid paying the former star the money owed to him. "Mario has done everything for the Pittsburgh Penguins," Reich said. "He has gone out of his way to accommodate them. But this is a contract that was signed by both parties and recognized by the NHL, as were all of the various revisions. That must be honored. Believe me: Mario will be paid."

In June 1998, Mario sued Marino and the Penguins for $32.5 million. Two companies who were owed money by the team, Spectacor Management Group and Fox Sports Pittsburgh, also took their matters to court. The Penguins' ownership was mired in a money mess. Baldwin and Marino were feuding; each wanted to buy the other's share in the team and become the controlling owner. But the money owed to Mario and others made the situation even more complicated. All through this time, the Penguins continued to lose more money. Eventually, the team filed for bankruptcy, which allows the court system to help find ways to pay off debts.

In October 1998, Mario was appointed by the government to cochair a group of creditors who were owed money by the Penguins. Mario and his fellow panel members would be able to work with the team in coming up with a plan to pay off its debts. In the succeeding 11 months, a plan was developed that had Mario taking control of the team. As the person owed the most money by the Penguins, Mario would receive most of his payment by becoming primary owner.

The alternative was for the Penguins to move to another city, where they could easily make more money. Mario didn't want that to happen. He had invested too much of his life and heart in the franchise to simply let it go broke and move. Pittsburgh was his home, and the Penguins were his team. Now, under this plan, the Penguins would literally be *his* team.

Taking advantage of his famous name and many contacts, Mario organized a group of investors who would take control of the Penguins. He would be the primary owner, the man in charge. On September 3, 1999, the plan was approved in bankruptcy court, making Mario the official owner.

One of Mario's first moves was to lower ticket prices for Penguins games, including special family deals. He wanted to get Pittsburgh fans excited about hockey once again. Shortly after the court ruling, a television commercial began airing that had Mario pictured in goaltender equipment. The advertisement listed the career statistics of the sixth-best scorer in NHL history: 613 goals, 881 assists, 1,494 points. Then, referring to the goalie gear, "One save." The reference, of course, was to Mario's having saved the Pittsburgh Penguins franchise. In the mid-1980s, he had done it as a player. Now, nearing the new millennium, he was doing it as an owner.

After approving the plan that transferred the team into

Mario exits the building where he submitted his proposal for purchasing the bankrupt Penguins. He would eventually become the primary owner of the club.

Mario's hands, bankruptcy judge Bernard Markovitz had said, "Now the puck is on Mr. Lemieux's stick. We've seen what he's been able to do with that."

But neither the judge nor anyone else expected to see him return to the ice.

On December 11, 2000, Mario announced to the world that he'd be returning to play for the Penguins. He felt that new rules had improved the game he missed so much.

11

THE MAGNIFICENT COMEBACK

IT WAS A Wednesday in early December, around five o'clock in the afternoon. This was about the time that most workers end their day, go home, and relax. For Kevin Allen, work was just beginning.

As the top hockey writer for *USA Today,* a big part of Allen's job was to keep in touch with important people around the National Hockey League: players, coaches, general managers, owners, other journalists. Through this string of contacts Allen collected all sorts of inside information. He knew about big trades before they happened. He learned of major contract deals before they were signed. Hockey people trusted him; they told Allen things they wouldn't share with other writers.

So as the clock struck five on this evening of December 6, 2000, Allen got a tip. As one of the best hockey writers in the business, Allen was respected around the league for his ability to break big news. But even for him, this was big—extremely big.

You might even say "Super." As in "Super Mario."

The information Allen received was that Mario, three and a half years after retiring, was about to return to the game. "The tip was at five o'clock in the evening," Allen said. "I went to a game, and during the game I thought about it and it made sense to me. I get a lot of those tips, but the tip in conjunction with everything that I knew, I knew something was right."

During the game, Allen considered all his information: He had heard whispers recently that the Penguins' owner had been skating at a Pittsburgh-area ice rink. People who had seen Mario recently commented that he had lost some weight. Back in September, Allen had interviewed Mario. "He said some things that were clues," Allen remembered. "He talked about how the game had changed. He talked about when he watches it, if it were still like this, he never would have quit. So there were some signs."

The next morning, Allen woke up at 7:30. He immediately started making phone calls, trying to figure out whether his hunch was correct. As he learned quickly, it was: Mario had begun gymnasium workouts in early November and started skating at the end of the month. With his information confirmed an hour later, Allen wrote the article that contained the biggest news in hockey that year: Mario Lemieux was making a comeback.

By 9 A.M. on Thursday, December 7, Allen's story was on the website of *USA Today*. The news was officially out, and radio stations, TV channels, and newspapers across the country picked it up. Everyone was shocked, even Mario's Penguins. Except for captain Jaromir Jagr, the players had known nothing about his comeback. The first they heard of it was on the radio in the locker room. "I still remember the first day when we heard it over the radio," said Bob Boughner, a defenseman for the Penguins. "It was the best-kept secret in town. We heard it on the radio while we were getting dressed for practice. All of us just looked at each other. We were in shock. It was disbelief."

Mario, always a quiet guy anyway, had done a great job of keeping his comeback a secret. A month earlier, he had gotten a Mellon Arena worker to help him secretly carry an exercise bike out of the Penguins' workout room when no one else was around. The rink where he worked out, Island Sports Center, was run by Kevin Constantine (a former NHL coach) and Dave Hanson (star of the hockey movie *Slap Shot*). His trainer was Jay Caufield, a former Penguin, and his workout mates included two more former team-mates, Dave Hannan and Bob Errey. The people who knew Mario was making a comeback shared the bond of being hockey men, and they were willing to keep a secret.

To get back into playing shape, Mario had to change his diet. He gave up food like fries and chicken fingers, replacing those with meat, fish, and vegetables. Tom Rooney, the Penguins' executive vice president, noticed that the food spread had changed inside the owner's suite during games at Mellon Arena. He shared that with reporters while introducing Mario on Monday, December 11, the date of the official press conference that announced the comeback. "People would ask, 'Were there any hints that he was coming back?' " Rooney said. "Well, for the first time in 15 months, a couple of weeks ago, we started not to see Mario in the morning. Evidently, he was working out and losing weight and the sign to me was when the chicken fingers went off the menu in the suite, I knew that something was coming up because vegetarian lasagna was something that he never used to eat."

At that press conference, Mario revealed his reasons for making a comeback. "I think the most important one is that I do miss the game tremendously," he said. "I think spending the last two years in the owner's box, having watched this team play for the last few years, I think we have a great young team that's got a lot of potential at this time. It is something that I'd like to be a part of once again."

For an athlete to come out of retirement is rare, but it certainly had happened before. Hockey legends Gordie Howe and Guy Lafleur had done it. So had basketball superstar Michael Jordan. The difference between them and

Mario, however, was that people had predicted it. Their comebacks were big news, but not shocking. Nobody, however, had expected Mario Lemieux to return to the ice. When he retired from the game at the end of the 1997 season, he said many times that he would never play again. "It's time to do something else with my life," he said.

Three and a half years earlier, Mario had been frustrated with the way hockey was being played. All the clutching and grabbing that happened in the neutral zone (the mid-ice area between the blue lines) was slowing down the game. Referees weren't calling penalties for this type of interference, and it was tripping up the ability of superstars like Mario to put on a dazzling show. The neutral zone is where great plays start: the puck is passed, skaters gain speed, and everything crashes toward the net in a showdown between shooters and a goalie. This kind of high-speed, fancy play is what made guys like Mario and Wayne Gretzky famous. But now, with teams playing a defensive style called the "neutral zone trap," the puck sort of dribbled around the ice while players wrestled to break free of each other. The game had become boring, and Mario wanted out.

"I won't miss the way the game's being played," Mario had said when he retired. But three and a half years later, the game had changed. Every game now had two referees, instead of one. By order of NHL commissioner Gary Bettman, his assistant Colin Campbell, and the director of officials, Andy VanHellemond, interference rules were being enforced much more strictly. This allowed the game to be played on wide-open ice, the perfect atmosphere for a superstar like Super Mario to thrive. "I think the game is going in the right direction," Mario said when announcing his comeback. "I know I was very critical at times of the game, and that was certainly one of the reasons why I left the game three years ago. But I do have to thank Mr. Bettman, Andy VanHellemond and Colin Campbell for the great job they have done turning around this sport. I think it is a lot more exciting now, not only for the players,

but also for the fans that are watching these games."

Mario's personal fan club—his family—would be a little bigger this time around. Mario and Nathalie had four kids now, and they were all old enough to see their dad play and remember it. Mario revealed his comeback plan to his kids the same day that the breaking story appeared on *USA*

Florida's Robert Svehla drills Mario during the 1996 NHL playoffs. Physical play was one of the reasons Mario left the game in 1997.

Today's website. "It was just a couple of days ago when they came home from school," Mario said. "The news was out on Thursday and I just told them that daddy was coming back to play with Jagr, and my son was really happy."

Mario made special mention of Austin, who was a huge hockey fan (his favorite player was Jagr) and had never seen his dad play. Austin was a miracle baby. He had been born three and a half months premature and seemingly had little chance of living. The fine care of doctors and nurses at his hospital allowed Austin to grow into a healthy little boy. "Austin is really the miracle child," said Kevin Allen. "I've been in Mario's house, I've sat with him as he's watched his kids. In Mario's house there's a picture, which I've seen hanging on the wall, of the child in the palm of his hand. That's how small he was."

Over the next three weeks that preceded Mario's comeback game, reporters across the country made a huge deal out of a father coming back to play in front of his son. Little Austin Lemieux became a celebrity, too, as he was filmed and photographed hanging around the locker room with his dad.

"He has certainly been a big part of my life since the day he was born," Mario said. "He's a young kid that gets up early in the morning with his hockey stick in his hands, loves the game of hockey, and I'm sure he would like to see his dad play before it's too late. So I feel that being 35 years old is not too late."

Some details needed to be worked out in order for Mario to be both a player and an owner at the same time. How much he paid himself could have an effect on teams across the league, because players often use the average salary when bargaining for new contracts. So that he didn't affect that number, Mario "hired" himself for the league average salary of $1.4 million per year. As an owner, he agreed not to participate in league decisions for as long as he is a player. (For instance, Mario will not vote at league meetings.) He left the day-to-day operations of the hockey club to Rooney and general manager Craig Patrick, who also was responsible for

Mario with his four-year-old son, Austin, after a practice. A great hockey fan whose favorite player was the Penguins' Jaromir Jagr, Austin eagerly anticipated seeing his father play in the NHL.

making trades. Still, Mario retained the right to make major decisions that would affect the team. "I want to go back to be a player, the way I was a few years ago," Mario said, "and that's going to take up 99 percent of my time."

Just the way it always had.

Returning hero: Mario acknowledges the fans after his first hockey game since emerging from a three-and-a-half-year retirement, December 27, 2000. Once again, he made his comeback memorable, scoring a goal and tallying two assists as the Penguins beat Toronto.

12

LIVING A DREAM

ON THE NIGHT Mario Lemieux made his historic comeback, nearly one million fans watched the game on television.

Jake Eck was not one of those million people. For sure, the nine-year-old hockey player was a Mario Lemieux fan. He had spent much of his young life living in Pittsburgh, hearing stories about the great Mario. Six months earlier, Jake and his family had moved from Pennsylvania to Virginia, but his allegiance to Mario continued: Jake carried all his hockey equipment in a tattered old bag emblazoned with the number 66. His parents would have been happy to buy him a newer, nicer bag, but this was the one Jake wanted.

As big a fan as Jake was, he had never seen Mario play hockey. When Mario retired, Jake was only 5. The night of December 27 would have been Jake's first chance to see his hero play. But the boy was fighting a battle that Mario knew well. One day earlier, Jake had undergone surgery to remove a cancerous tumor from beneath his skull. So on the Wednesday night that brought Mario back to hockey, Jake was recovering in his hospital bed. He had wanted to watch the Penguins-Maple Leafs game, but the Virginia hospital didn't get the right channel on the television.

That night, Jake's parents, Jim and Missy, came into his room to tell him that Mario had scored a goal and added two assists and that the Penguins had won. "He was pretty excited," Missy remembered, and Jake had good reason to feel happy: both he and his hero, a fan and a legend, were on their way to overcoming huge obstacles.

In the days leading up to December 27, Mario had been practicing with his Penguins teammates. Jake, meanwhile, had been leading the normal life of a fourth-grader. For him, that all changed a few days before Christmas. "Jake had started getting headaches, saying, 'My head is killing me,'" Missy said. "He took Tylenol and was fine, but got more headaches the next day and started throwing up."

At first, doctors told Jake's parents that he probably had a sinus infection and gave him antibiotics. But over the next two days, the symptoms worsened: Jake couldn't tolerate light or noise. He was sleeping most of the day and night, and when he woke up, he would vomit. His eyes were twitching. When he talked, his words didn't make any sense.

Understandably alarmed, Jim and Missy brought Jake to an emergency room, where doctors performed a CAT scan. That is when they discovered a tumor growing on his brain, located behind his right ear. Jake spent Christmas Eve and Christmas Day in the hospital. Some of his symptoms were improving, but fluid was building up inside his head and causing unbearable pressure. To fix that, doctors had to drill a hole into Jake's skull and insert a temporary shunt to drain the fluid. On December 26, they performed the surgery to remove the tumor, called a medulloblastoma. Doctors told the Ecks that Jake would need to be treated with radiation therapy on his head and spine to make sure that no cancerous cells remained on his brain or in his spinal fluid. Over the next several months, Jake would also need to undergo eight 42-day cycles of chemotherapy.

They also said that with this type of cancer, which affects roughly 1,000 kids per year, there is an 80 percent survival rate. "I said to the doctor, 'I can't believe we have to do this to him,' " Missy said, "because he seemed fine. The doctor said, 'If you don't do it, he will die.' "

Jake left the hospital and returned home on Thursday, December 28, one day after Mario's comeback game. As he recovered from surgery, returned to school, and prepared for radiation and chemotherapy treatments, Jake also had the chance to finally watch Mario play. Over the next few months, Mario put on a show worth watching: in his first eight games, he scored nine goals. ESPN covered his first five games and, thanks in small part to Jake, had a 45 percent jump in viewer ratings.

As expected, Mario was picked to play in the All-Star Game and was named captain of the North American team. During the festivities in Denver, he announced his plans to play during the 2001–02 season, and maybe even longer. "I'm going to play as long as my body allows me to," he said. At that point in early February, Mario had played in every game since returning. (Later that season, he would sit out three different games to rest his back.) With 32 points in 16 games, he astounded even his fellow All-Stars. "I figured he would eventually average two points a game," said New York Rangers defenseman Brian Leetch, "but already? No, I'm surprised. It's amazing. I'm like everybody else right now, going to the sports pages or watching the highlights every night to see how many he got that night."

In the All-Star Game, Mario scored one goal and assisted on another to help the North American team beat the World stars, 14-12. Reporters started comparing this comeback to others Mario had made, including his 1993 return from cancer. "This one is easier because I had a fresh start," Mario said. "I was healthy. My back was in great shape. I didn't have to go through radiation for six weeks and be depleted physically and mentally."

Though the disease was in his past, Mario remembered

exactly how difficult it was to absorb cancer treatment. Radiation and chemotherapy, though designed to kill lethal cancer cells, can also make you feel sick and can cause you to lose your hair. Mario's cancer and his treatment had been relatively mild compared with what someone like Jake was going through, which makes what happened on March 29, 2001, all the more inspiring.

Just 48 hours earlier, on a Monday, the Eck family had gotten a phone call from the Make A Wish Foundation, asking them if they would be able to go to Pittsburgh the next day. The Make A Wish representative told them that they could bring the entire family to Tuesday night's Penguins-Sabres game and, the next morning, Jake would get to skate with Mario Lemieux. The Ecks were actually on vacation in Florida at the time, but they packed up and went home to Virginia. On Tuesday morning, Jake traveled to Pittsburgh along with his mom, dad, six-year-old brother Joe, and five-year-old sister Maggie. "That was one of those once-in-a-lifetime things," Jim Eck, Jake's dad, said, "so you push everything aside and do what's important."

On the evening of March 27, Jake not only saw his hero play hockey, he witnessed Mario in superstar form, recording two assists as Pittsburgh beat Buffalo, 4-1. Jake wasn't the only one watching in awe that night. Sabres rookie J. P. Dumont, who grew up in French-speaking Quebec and considered Mario his hero, was playing against number 66 for the first time. Mario was one of the few athletes in the NHL who could actually mesmerize his opponents and make them talk like fans. "When I found out that he was making a comeback, I went and looked at the schedule to see when we'd be playing Pittsburgh," Dumont said. "I've been waiting for this game with excitement. I'd like to meet him, maybe at the morning skate. But he's a big star, really big in Quebec. If I were to meet him, I wonder if I'd even be able to talk to him."

It would be another six weeks before Dumont shook Mario's hand. Jake's time would come much sooner. The next day, the Penguins had a noon practice at Mellon Arena. Jake and his family sat close to the ice, right next to the players' walkway. As coach Ivan Hlinka led his team through a variety of drills to practice their new left-wing lock defensive system, Jake and his brother Joe ran up and down the rows of seats behind goalie Jean-Sebastien Aubin, collecting pucks that had flown over the glass. On top of his shirt and tie, Jake was wearing a Mario jersey. He covered his head with a Penguins baseball cap. About one hour into practice, Mario skated over to the ice entrance, where Jake was waiting with his hockey skates. "Are you ready?" he asked Jake.

With his stick in hand, Jake began to step onto the ice. Mario stopped him, smiled, and pointed to Jake's feet. He had forgotten to remove his skate guards! Quickly, Jake pulled off the plastic straps that covered his skate blades and stepped onto the ice, following the real number 66. As Jake and Mario began passing the puck back and forth, sports reporters watched the scene from the stands, making comments like, "Man, that kid can skate!" and "Hey, maybe Mario is getting a new linemate!" Jim Eck taped the whole scene, from the fast-paced passing exercises to the tic-tac-toe shooting drills. At one point, Mario passed the puck to Jake, who skated on a breakaway toward Aubin in goal. As Jake moved the puck from side to side, Aubin shifted himself from left to right, wildly animating his actions. Jake reared back and shot the puck toward the net. Aubin made a slow-motion lunge for the puck, sprawling to the ice as the shot sank into the net. Jake had scored on an NHL goalie! Led by Mario, all the Penguins who were watching tapped their sticks to the ice in applause. "He's getting pretty good," Mario told reporters after practice. "He has a good shot."

Jake loved the compliment, but wasn't fooled into thinking he was ready to play next to Mario. Not yet, at least. "I think he was going easy on me," Jake said. "He wasn't doing anything real hard."

Nine-year-old cancer survivor Jake Eck poses with his idol. Jake skated with Mario during a March 2001 Penguins practice.

After the practice, Mario took Jake and his brother and father into the Penguins locker room. He gave them a tour of the entire facility, which included an equipment area and a dressing room with big black leather couches, a wide-screen television, and a refrigerator full of sports drinks. One by one, Mario introduced Jake to all his Penguins teammates.

Mario signed Jake's jersey: "To Jake—Best of luck. Your friend, Mario Lemieux." Jake had something for Mario, too. He pulled out a picture of himself wearing his Mario jersey and holding a stick and a signed picture of

Mario. (When Jake had become sick, a friend of his father had gotten him a signed Mario stick. At the same time, Jake's great-aunt called the Penguins to get a signed Mario photograph.) For his new friend, Jake autographed the photograph of himself: "To my hero Mario, Jake Eck." When Jake handed it to him, Mario put the picture up in his locker.

Jake, who had recently begun playing hockey again, told Mario about his first game back from radiation. "I scored four goals," Jake said.

"Oh man, you did better than me," Mario replied. "I only scored one goal in my first game back from radiation."

For Mario, of course, that was two comebacks ago. Making grand returns to hockey had become a way of life for him, and he was happy to share his story with people who needed to hear it. People like Jake. "It's the least I can do to try to help these young kids get through some tough times," Mario said. "I've been through it in the past, and it's not easy, physically and especially mentally. So if I can make a kid happy for a couple hours and give him some words of encouragement, have him think about the future and not the present, that's really all I can do."

With their owner now a teammate, the Penguins' future was looking better, too. Team management, especially Mario, was looking to make a deal to build a new arena in Pittsburgh. But for that to happen, the Penguins needed to prove they could be a winning, and financially stable, team. Mario did his part, registering 35 goals and 41 assists in 43 games. With the boss in the lineup, the Penguins had a record of 26 wins, 12 losses, and three ties. They finished the season third in the Atlantic Division with 96 points, which meant they would face the Washington Capitals in the first round of the playoffs.

After losing the first game versus Washington, Pittsburgh won four of the next five and advanced to the second round. Their opponent was the Buffalo Sabres, who looked like they would be easy fodder for the

A savvy businessman as well as a hockey superstar, Mario is seen here publicizing an Internet venture with which he is involved.

Cup-hungry Penguins. Pittsburgh won the first two games, 3-0 and 3-1, in Buffalo. But back in Pittsburgh, the Penguins fell apart as Buffalo won the next two and evened the series. Each of the final three games went into overtime, with Pittsburgh winning game seven, 3-2.

This time, Sabres rookie J. P. Dumont did get to meet his hero. After game seven, Dumont shook Mario's hand. "That was great to play against my hero," Dumont said. "Where I am from, he's probably the most popular guy ever. Not just in sports, but in almost everything back in

Montreal. It was just great to have the chance to play against him. It's too bad I didn't have the chance to beat him. But it was great, and after the series it was an honor to shake his hand, too."

Dumont didn't say much to Mario, just "Bonne chance." In French that means "Good luck." Dumont knew Mario was headed to the Eastern Conference Finals, in which Pittsburgh played the New Jersey Devils. The Devils, the defending Stanley Cup champions, dominated the Penguins in the series, beating them in five games. The Devils scored 19 goals in the series; the Penguins recorded just 5. "It's been a great ride to come back after three and a half years," Mario said. "I wanted to go to the Finals and get another chance to win the Stanley Cup, but it wasn't to be."

Not in 2001, anyway. Whether or not Mario ever wins another Stanley Cup, he will be remembered as a player who overcame every obstacle in his path. He has already overcome a language barrier, back problems, and cancer.

As Jake Eck was fighting his own battle against cancer, he kept reminding himself of Mario's return. "The best player in the world had cancer," Jake told himself, "and he came back to play hockey." No lesson could have been learned better.

"I'm a perfect example that there's life after cancer," Mario said. "I was able to fight through it and get back on the ice and live a normal life."

CAREER STATISTICS

REGULAR SEASON*

YEAR	TM	GP	G	A	PTS	PIM	+/–	PPA	PPG	SHG	SHA	SHOTS	PCT
1984-85	Pit	73	43	57	100	54	-35	22	11	0	—	209	20.6
1985-86	Pit	79	48	93	141	43	-6	45	17	0	—	276	17.4
1986-87	Pit	63	54	53	107	57	13	19	19	0	—	267	20.2
1987-88	Pit	77	70	98	168	92	23	58	22	10	—	382	18.3
1988-89	Pit	76	85	114	199	100	41	49	31	13	—	313	27.2
1989-90	Pit	59	45	78	123	78	-18	35	14	3	—	226	19.9
1990-91	Pit	26	19	26	45	30	8	8	6	1	0	89	21.3
1991-92	Pit	64	44	87	131	94	27	35	12	4	6	249	17.7
1992-93	Pit	60	69	91	160	38	55	39	16	6	3	286	24.1
1993-94	Pit	22	17	20	37	32	-2	8	7	0	0	92	18.5
1995-96	Pit	70	69	92	161	54	10	48	31	8	1	338	20.4
1996-97	Pit	76	50	72	122	65	27	22	15	2	3	327	15.3
2000-01	Pit	43	35	41	76	18	15	16	16	1	0	171	20.5
Totals		**788**	**648**	**922**	**1570**	**755**	**217**	**158**	**404**	**48**	—	**3225**	**20.1**

POST SEASON*

YEAR	TM	GP	G	A	PTS	PIM
1984-85	Pit	—	—	—	—	—
1985-86	Pit	—	—	—	—	—
1986-87	Pit	—	—	—	—	—
1987-88	Pit	—	—	—	—	—
1988-89	Pit	11	12	7	19	16
1989-90	Pit	—	—	—	—	—
1990-91	Pit	23	16	28	44	16
1991-92	Pit	15	16	18	34	2
1992-93	Pit	11	8	10	18	10
1993-94	Pit	6	4	3	7	2
1995-96	Pit	18	11	16	27	33
1996-97	Pit	5	3	3	6	4
2000-01	Pit	18	6	11	17	4
Totals		**107**	**76**	**96**	**172**	**87**

KEY

GP	games played
G	goals
A	assists
PIM	penalties in minutes
+/–	plus/minus rating
PPA	power-play assists
PPG	power-play goals
SHG	short-handed goals
SHA	short-handed assists

through April 7, 2001

CHRONOLOGY

1965   Mario Lemieux is born on October 5 in the Montreal village of Ville Emard.

1968   At age 3, begins playing pickup hockey.

1971–1980   Plays organized hockey in the Montreal area. Coaches and fans quickly recognize his superstar potential.

1981–84   Plays for the Laval Voisins of the Quebec Major Junior Hockey League. In 1982, also plays for Canada in the world junior championships in the Soviet Union.

1984–85   Picked first overall in the National Hockey League draft (June 19, 1984) by the Pittsburgh Penguins. Debuts on October 11, 1984, in Boston and scores on his first shot. Finishes the season with 100 points and is named rookie of the year. Plays in the world championships in Czechoslovakia after the season.

1985–86   Records 141 points, finishing second to Wayne Gretzky in the Hart Trophy (most valuable player) voting and the scoring race. Wins the Lester B. Pearson Award (best player) from the NHL Players' Association.

1986–87   Misses 13 games with a sprained right knee and still leads team with 54 goals and 53 assists for 107 points. Teams with Wayne Gretzky and several other Canadian-born superstars to lead his country's team to a world championship in the Canada Cup tournament during the summer of '87.

1987–88   Wins the Art Ross Trophy (league-leading scorer) with 70 goals and 98 assists for 168 points. Also wins the Hart Trophy and Lester B. Pearson Award.

1988–89   Wins the Art Ross Trophy (85 goals and 114 assists for 199 points).

1989–90   Embarks on a 46-game scoring streak (October 31 to February 14, scoring 39 goals and 64 assists). Misses the next 21 games with back problems.

1990–91   Undergoes corrective back surgery on July 11, 1990, and misses the first 50 games of the season, returning on January 26. Leads the Penguins to a Stanley Cup championship. Awarded the Conn Smythe Trophy (playoff MVP).

1991–92   Back problems limit him to 64 games. Wins his third scoring championship (131 points). Pittsburgh wins a second straight Stanley Cup; Mario wins the Conn Smythe Trophy.

1992–93   Announces on January 12, 1993, that he has been diagnosed with Hodgkin's disease; misses 20 games in midseason to undergo radiation therapy. In 60 games, scores 160 points. Wins four major awards: Art Ross Trophy, Hart Trophy, Lester B. Pearson Award, and Masterton Trophy. First child (Lauren) is born on April 29. Marries Nathalie Asselin on June 26 in Montreal.

CHRONOLOGY

1993–94 Misses 60 games while suffering from back problems. Season totals (17 goals, 20 assists, 37 points) are career lows. Expresses frustration that NHL officials are not properly enforcing interference penalties.

1994–95 Announces on August 29 that he will sit out the entire season to recuperate from back injuries and fatigue. Announces on June 20 that he will return for the 1995–96 season.

1995–96 Wins Hart Trophy and Art Ross Trophy with 161 points (69 goals, 92 assists). Scores his 500th career goal on October 28.

1996–97 Wins Art Ross Trophy (50 goals, 72 assists, 122 points). Scores his 600th goal on February 4. Retires at the close of the season, which ends on April 26, 1997, as Philadelphia eliminates Pittsburgh in the first round of the playoffs.

1997 Inducted into the Hockey Hall of Fame on November 17. Jersey is retired by the Pittsburgh Penguins on November 18.

1998 Owed approximately $30 million in pay by the Pittsburgh Penguins. The team, which is losing money and in debt to creditors, files for bankruptcy.

1999 Organizes a group of investors to take control of the Penguins. On September 3, a bankruptcy judge puts the team in the group's hands, making Mario the controlling owner.

2000–01 On December 27, he plays his first game after a three-and-a-half-year absence. That spring, the Penguins make it to the Eastern Conference Finals, but lose to New Jersey.

FURTHER READING

Cox, Ted. *Sports Stars: Mario Lemieux: Super Mario*. Chicago: Children's Press, 1993.

Hughes, Morgan E. *Mario Lemieux: Beating the Odds*. Minneapolis: Lerner Publications Company, 1996.

Klein, Jeff Z. *Great Achievers: Lives of the Physically Challenged—Mario Lemieux*. Philadelphia: Chelsea House Publishers, 1999.

Knapp, Ron. *Sports Great: Mario Lemieux*. Springfield, N.J.: Enslow Publishers, Inc., 1995.

Lemieux, Mario. *The Final Period*. Pittsburgh: Reich, Brisson and Reich Publishing, Inc., 1997.

Martin, Lawrence. *Mario*. Toronto: Lester, 1993.

Molinari, Dave. *Best in the Game: The Turbulent Story of the Pittsburgh Penguins' Rise to Stanley Cup Champions*. Chicago: Sagamore Publishing, 1993.

Rappoport, Ken. *Sports Reports: Mario Lemieux*. Springfield, N.J.: Enslow Publishers, Inc., 1998.

Tarcy, Brian. *Ice Hockey Legends: Mario Lemieux*. Philadelphia: Chelsea House Publishers, 2001.

INDEX

PICTURE CREDITS

Tim O'Shei's dad took him to his first NHL game the same season (1984–85) that Mario Lemieux entered the league. He was eight years old at the time and began covering the Buffalo Sabres a decade later. As a freelance writer, Tim has covered the NHL and NFL for a variety of national magazines. He has written several books for young readers on sports, music, and history. Tim is also a teacher and runs writing workshops for young authors. In his free time, he enjoys running, listening to music, playing the tuba, and watching television (CNN, MTV, and ESPN). You can visit his website at www.writepages.com.

James Scott Brady serves on the board of trustees with the Center to Prevent Handgun Violence and is the vice chairman of the Brain Injury Foundation. Mr. Brady served as assistant to the President and White House press secretary under President Ronald Reagan. He was severely injured in an assassination attempt on the president, but remained the White House press secretary until the end of the administration. Since leaving the White House, Mr. Brady has lobbied for stronger gun laws. In November 1993, President Bill Clinton signed the Brady Bill, a national law requiring a waiting period on handgun purchases and a background check on buyers.